Networks Social Studies

Who We Are as Americans

Teacher Edition

The White House

Mc
Graw
Hill
Education

PROGRAM AUTHORS

James A. Banks, Ph.D.
Kerry and Linda Killinger Endowed
  Chair in Diversity Studies and
  Director, Center for Multicultural
  Education
University of Washington
Seattle, Washington

Kevin P. Colleary, Ed.D.
Curriculum and Teaching Department
Graduate School of Education
Fordham University
New York, New York

Linda Greenow, Ph.D.
Associate Professor and Chair
Department of Geography
State University of New York at
  New Paltz
New Paltz, New York

Walter C. Parker, Ph.D.
Professor of Social Studies Education,
  Adjunct Professor of Political
  Science
University of Washington
Seattle, Washington

Emily M. Schell, Ed.D.
Visiting Professor, Teacher Education
San Diego State University
San Diego, California

Dinah Zike
Educational Consultant
Dinah-Might Adventures, L.P.
San Antonio, Texas

CONTRIBUTING AUTHORS

James M. Denham, Ph.D.
Professor of History and Director,
  Lawton M. Chiles, Jr., Center for
  Florida History
Florida Southern College
Lakeland, Florida

M.C. Bob Leonard, Ph.D.
Professor, Hillsborough Community
  College
Director, Florida History Internet Center
Ybor City, Florida

Jay McTighe
Educational Author and Consultant
McTighe and Associates Consulting
Columbia, Maryland

Timothy Shanahan, Ph.D.
Professor of Urban Education &
  Director, Center for Literacy
College of Education
University of Illinois at Chicago

ACADEMIC CONSULTANTS

Tom Daccord
Educational Technology Specialist
Co-Director, EdTechTeacher
Boston, Massachusetts

Joe Follman
Service Learning Specialist
Director, Florida Learn & Serve

Cathryn Berger Kaye, M.A.
Service Learning Specialist
Author, *The Complete Guide to
  Service Learning*

Justin Reich
Educational Technology Specialist
Co-Director, EdTechTeacher
Boston, Massachusetts

Send all inquiries to:
McGraw-Hill Education
8787 Orion Place
Columbus, OH 43240

ISBN: 978-0-02-144929-3
MHID: 0-02-144929-5

Printed in the United States of America.

1 2 3 4 5 6 7 8 9 QVS 18 17 16 15 14

Common Core State Standards© Copyright 2010. National Governors Association Center for Best Practices and Council of Chief State School Officers. All rights reserved.

Understanding by Design® is a registered trademark of the Association for Supervision and Curriculum Development ("ASCD").

Table of Contents

UNIT 1 Our World

BIG IDEA 💡 Maps help us understand the world.

UNIT 2 Native Americans

BIG IDEA 💡 Culture influences the way people live.

UNIT 3 A Land of Immigrants

BIG IDEA 💡 Change happens over time.

UNIT 4 Citizens and Government

BIG IDEA 💡 People's actions affect others.

Notebook FOLDABLES® templates can be found at the end of this Teacher Edition.

Table of Contents

UNIT 5 All About Economics

BIG IDEA 💡 Relationships affect choices.

Skills and Maps

Notebook FOLDABLES templates can be found at the end of this Teacher Edition.

Networks Social Studies

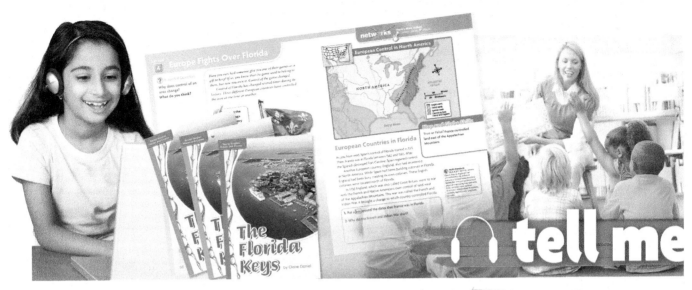

tell me

show me

involve me

Start networking!

connected.mcgraw-hill.com

Teacher Planning

Planning pages appear at the beginning of each unit.

• Unit Big Idea

The Big Idea is the major theme that helps students organize and understand information.

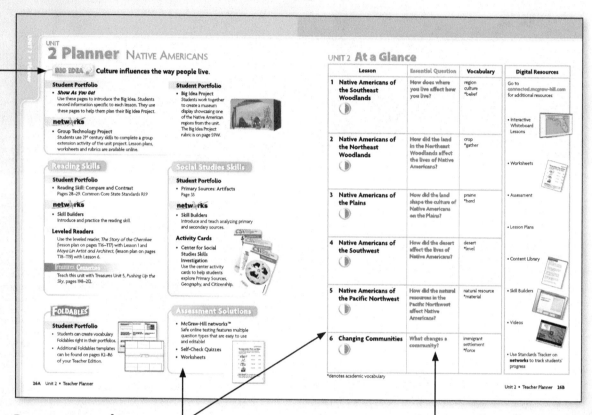

Resources and Lessons at a Glance •

Planning made easy.

• Essential Questions

Lesson-specific Essential Questions tie content to the Unit Big Idea.

Start netw rking!

Customizable Model Lesson Plans

The online teacher edition features model lesson plans for each lesson. You can customize each lesson plan to fit your time demands and the needs of your students.

Understanding by Design®

Quality instruction develops and deepens student understanding through the use of carefully crafted learning experiences. The **McGraw-Hill networks™** program focuses on teaching for understanding through on-going, inquiry-based instruction and assessment. This program was created through the Understanding by Design® (UbD) curriculum design model. At the core of UbD lies a focus on what is taught and how it is assessed.

In the **networks** program, each unit is centered on a **Big Idea**. The unit Big Idea focuses student learning through the use of prior knowledge and stimulates deeper understanding.

The end of each unit features a **Big Idea Project**. Through this authentic assessment, students demonstrate the understanding gained within the unit. As a final step, students reflect and explain how what they learned affected their understanding of the Big Idea.

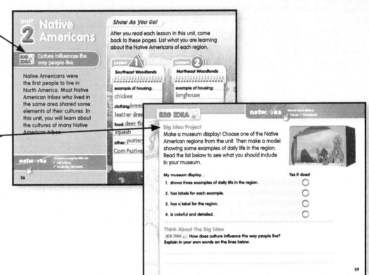

Each lesson focuses on an **Essential Question**. These open-ended questions allow students the opportunity to make connections, view events from different perspectives, and integrate information.

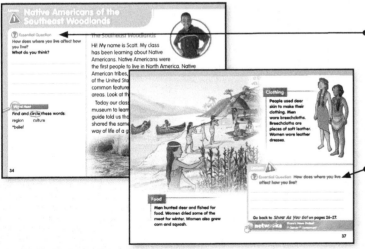

At the end of each lesson, students again respond to the **Essential Question**. This response should reflect a change in student understanding based on their experiences within the lesson.

Contributing Author

Jay McTighe has published articles in a number of leading educational journals and has co-authored ten books, including the best-selling *Understanding By Design* series with Grant Wiggins. Jay also has an extensive background in professional development and is a featured speaker at national, state, and district conferences and workshops. He received his undergraduate degree from The College of William and Mary, earned a Masters degree from The University of Maryland, and completed post-graduate studies at The Johns Hopkins University.

Student Engagement

Each lesson has activities that stimulate learning and interest.

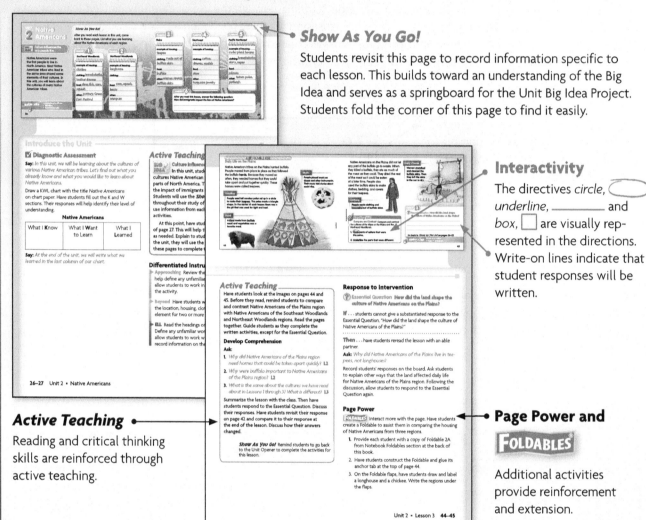

Show As You Go!

Students revisit this page to record information specific to each lesson. This builds toward an understanding of the Big Idea and serves as a springboard for the Unit Big Idea Project. Students fold the corner of this page to find it easily.

Interactivity

The directives *circle*, ⟨⟩ *underline*, _____ and *box*, ☐ are visually represented in the directions. Write-on lines indicate that student responses will be written.

Active Teaching

Reading and critical thinking skills are reinforced through active teaching.

Page Power and

FOLDABLES

Additional activities provide reinforcement and extension.

Start networking!

Interactive Whiteboard Lessons

Engage students with these interactive whiteboard activities. vLessons include images, vocabulary, and graphic organizers to enrich and extend Social Studies content. The vLessons and these additional digital resources motivate students and reinforce Social Studies concepts and skills:

• Interactive Maps
• Videos

Reading Integration

Each unit has skills-based instruction that focuses on Common Core State Standards for English Language Arts: Reading Standards for Informational Text.

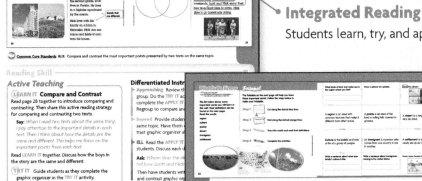

Integrated Reading and Writing Skills

Students learn, try, and apply the skills.

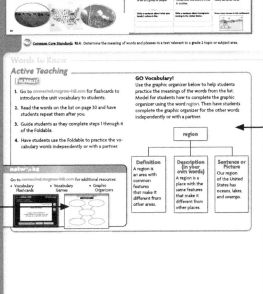

Vocabulary Foldable

After constructing the "stay in the book" Vocabulary Foldable, students complete activities that reinforce word meanings.

Vocabulary Instruction

Content and Academic Vocabulary are taught and reinforced through Foldables, graphic organizers, and games.

Graphic Organizers

Each unit has a different graphic organizer to help students gain a deeper understanding of unit vocabulary and concepts.

Start netw⊕rking!

Interactive Games

Engaging interactive Vocabulary Games help students practice vocabulary and concepts.

The Vocabulary Games and these additional digital resources can be used to introduce and review vocabulary, to reinforce reading skills, and to build comprehension and fluency:

- Vocabulary Flashcards
- Puzzle Maker
- Worksheets
- Graphic Organizers
- Skill Builders
- Audio-Visual Online Student Experience

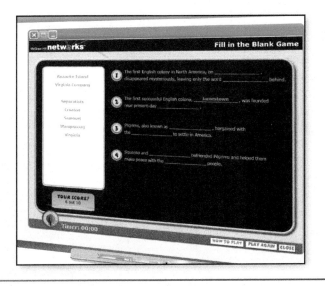

Social Studies Instruction

Skills instruction is spiraled throughout each grade and between grade levels.

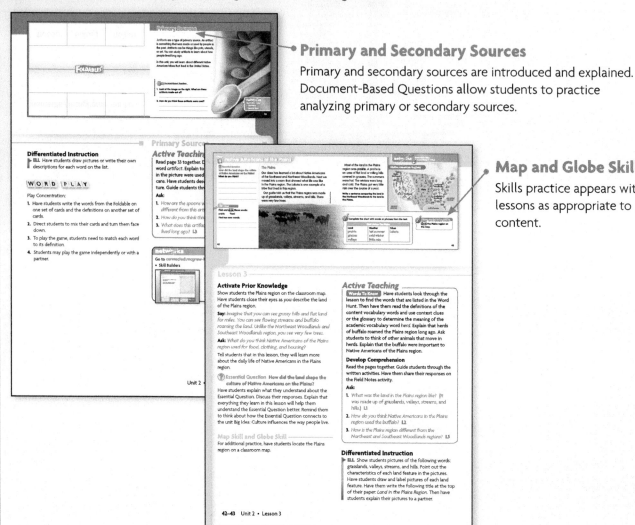

Primary and Secondary Sources

Primary and secondary sources are introduced and explained. Document-Based Questions allow students to practice analyzing primary or secondary sources.

Map and Globe Skills

Skills practice appears within lessons as appropriate to content.

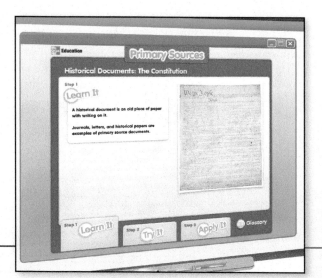

Start networking!

Skill Builders

Interactive learning tools help students use a variety of Social Studies skills. Each tool will allow students to learn, try, and apply each Social Studies skill in an active and engaging way.

- Primary Sources
- Map and Globe Skills
- Chart and Graph Skills

Project and Assessment

Each unit provides a variety of formative and summative assessments, as well as suggested interventions.

Essential Question

Students respond to the Essential Question using lesson content to support their response. This check provides an opportunity to redirect or intervene for struggling students.

Unit Wrap Up

Activities review and reinforce unit vocabulary and content.

Big Idea Project

Unit performance tasks require students to synthesize information while creating, presenting, and evaluating a project. Students use a checklist as a guide for working through the project. Each project has a reproducible project rubric for scoring.

Depths of Knowledge

Questions are leveled according to Depths of Knowledge.

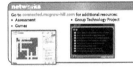

Response To Intervention

Provides intervention options for struggling students.

Start networking!

Self-Check Quizzes

Self-Check Quizzes gauge students' level of understanding before, during, or after studying a lesson. The Self-Check Quizzes and these additional resources are available for formative, summative, or project-based assessment.

• McGraw-Hill networks™ Assessment
• Group Technology Project

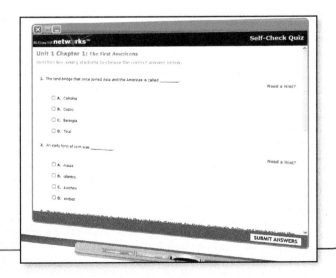

Differentiated Instruction

Differentiated instruction activities meet the diverse needs of every student.

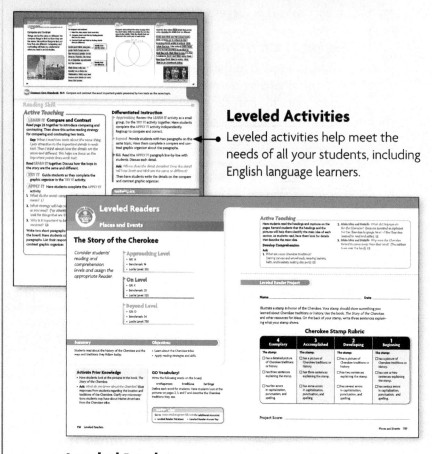

Leveled Activities

Leveled activities help meet the needs of all your students, including English language learners.

Center Card Activity Kit

Students investigate Primary Sources, Geography, and Citizenship.

Leveled Readers

One topic presented at three different reading levels provides an opportunity for your whole class to participate in a discussion about the topic.

Start networking!

- ## Content Library

  There's more to learn in the Content Library! A bank of short articles provides background information about topics covered in each unit. Use the Content Library to enrich or extend student knowledge beyond information presented in the text.

- ## Access Points

  Access Points activities for standards are available in your customizable model lesson plans. Here you will find independent, supported, and participatory activities to meet the needs of your students.

- ## Character Education

  Develop the character of your students with our Character Education curriculum. Students have the opportunity to explain, explore, experience, and exhibit a variety of character traits through cooperative activities and self-reflection.

- ## Service Learning

  Make Service Learning simple and easy with step-by-step guidance to enrich the learning experience of your students. Use hands-on, real-world projects to develop skills, behaviors, and habits of good citizenship.

Levels of Cognitive Complexity

Questions throughout your Teacher Edition are labeled L1 (Level 1), L2 (Level 2), or L3 (Level 3) depending upon their level of complexity.

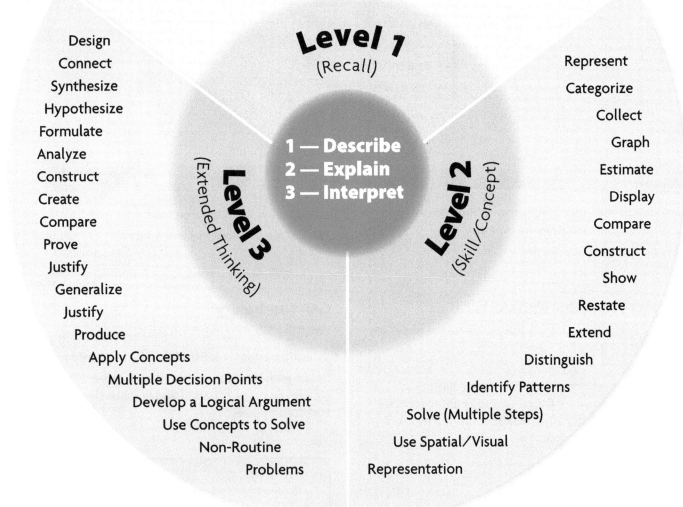

Draw
List

Identify
Recognize
Compute
Define

Retrieve
Procedure
State
Measure

Match
Recite
Tell
Name

Recall
Solve (1 Step)

Level 1
(Recall)

Design
Connect
Synthesize
Hypothesize
Formulate
Analyze
Construct
Create
Compare
Prove
Justify
Generalize
Justify
Produce
Apply Concepts
Multiple Decision Points
Develop a Logical Argument
Use Concepts to Solve
Non-Routine
Problems

Level 3
(Extended Thinking)

1 — Describe
2 — Explain
3 — Interpret

Level 2
(Skill/Concept)

Represent
Categorize
Collect
Graph
Estimate
Display
Compare
Construct
Show
Restate
Extend
Distinguish
Identify Patterns
Solve (Multiple Steps)
Use Spatial/Visual
Representation

Leveled Readers

Places and Events

The Story of the Cherokee

Consider students' reading and comprehension levels and assign the appropriate Reader.

Approaching Level
- GR: H
- Benchmark: 14
- Lexile Level: 330

On Level
- GR: K
- Benchmark: 20
- Lexile Level: 520

Beyond Level
- GR: O
- Benchmark: 34
- Lexile Level: 730

Summary

Students read about the history of the Cherokee and the ways and traditions they follow today.

Objectives

- Learn about the Cherokee tribe.
- Apply reading strategies and skills.

Activate Prior Knowledge

- Have students look at the pictures in the book, *The Story of the Cherokee.*
- **Ask:** *What do you know about the Cherokee?* Elicit responses from students regarding the location and traditions of the Cherokee. Clarify any misconceptions students may have about Native Americans from the Cherokee tribe.

GO Vocabulary!

Write the following words on the board.

craftsperson   traditions   heritage

Define each word for students. Have students look at the pictures on pages 2, 3, and 7 and describe the Cherokee traditions they see.

networks

Go to connected.mcgraw-hill.com for additional resources:
- Leveled Reader Database
- Leveled Reader Answer Key

Active Teaching

Have students read the headings and captions on the pages. Remind students that the headings and the pictures will help them identify the main idea of each section. As students read, have them look for details that describe the main idea.

Develop Comprehension

Ask:

1. *What are some Cherokee traditions?* (carving canoes and arrowheads, weaving baskets, belts, and blankets, making clay pots) **L2**

2. **Main Idea and Details** *What did Sequoya do for the Cherokee?* (Sequoya invented an alphabet for the Cherokee language. Most of the Cherokee learned to read and write.) **L2**

3. **Main Idea and Details** *Why were the Cherokee forced to move away from their land?* (The settlers took over the land.) **L2**

Leveled Reader Project

Name _____ Date _____

Illustrate a stamp in honor of the Cherokee. Your stamp should show something you learned about Cherokee traditions or history. Use the book, *The Story of the Cherokee*, and other resources for ideas. On the back of your stamp, write three sentences explaining what your stamp shows.

Cherokee Stamp Rubric

4 Exemplary	3 Accomplished	2 Developing	1 Beginning
The stamp:	**The stamp:**	**The stamp:**	**The stamp:**
☐ has a detailed picture of Cherokee traditions or history.	☐ has a picture of Cherokee traditions or history.	☐ has a picture of Cherokee traditions or history.	☐ has a picture of Cherokee traditions or history.
☐ has three sentences explaining the stamp.	☐ has three sentences explaining the stamp.	☐ has two sentences explaining the stamp.	☐ has one or two sentences explaining the stamp.
☐ has few errors in capitalization, punctuation, and spelling.	☐ has some errors in capitalization, punctuation, and spelling.	☐ has several errors in capitalization, punctuation, and spelling.	☐ has serious errors in capitalization, punctuation, and spelling.

Project Score: _____

SOCIAL STUDIES
Leveled Reader Library

Maya Lin, Artist And Architect

Consider students' reading and comprehension levels and assign the appropriate Reader.

▶ Approaching Level
- GR: F
- Benchmark: 10
- Lexile Level: 320

▶ On Level
- GR: L
- Benchmark: 24
- Lexile Level: 650

▶ Beyond Level
- GR: O
- Benchmark: 34
- Lexile Level: 700

Summary

Children read about the life of Maya Lin, how she became an artist and architect, and designed the memorials that honor Vietnam War veterans and civil rights activists.

Objectives

- Apply unit reading strategies and skills.
- Learn how artists make communities better places.

Activate Prior Knowledge

- Have children name a building that they like. Explain that an architect plans what a building looks like and how it is constructed. He or she draws a plan called a *design* before a building is built. Ask children to preview the reader's cover, table of contents, illustrations and first two sections of text to make predictions about the events in the story. Ask: *"What do the pictures tell us about Maya Lin?"*

GO Vocabulary!

Teach the vocabulary using the glossary in the back of the book. On the board, write some of the vocabulary terms from the reader. (*architect, design, memorial*) As a class, invite children to predict the meanings. Then help them locate the word and definition in the glossary.

networks

Go to **connected.mcgraw-hill.com** for additional resources:
- Leveled Reader Database
- Leveled Reader Answer Key

Active Teaching

Remind children that when they identify the main idea, they think about what a paragraph is mainly about. Point out that details tell more about the main idea.

Develop Comprehension

Ask:
1. *Why did Maya Lin become an artist?* **L1**
2. *What memorials did Maya Lin design?* **L2**
3. *Why is Maya Lin's work important?* **L2**

Leveled Reader Project

Name _____ **Date** _____

Imagine you are making a movie about Maya Lin. Create a storyboard with pictures for the movie. Draw pictures to show about events in Maya Lin's life. Add captions to explain what is happening in each storyboard picture.

Storyboard Rubric

4 Exemplary	3 Accomplished	2 Developing	1 Beginning
The storyboard: ☐ has five or more pictures showing events in Maya Lin's life. ☐ has captions for each picture.	The storyboard: ☐ has four pictures showing events in Maya Lin's life. ☐ has several captions for the pictures.	The storyboard: ☐ has three pictures showing events in Maya Lin's life. ☐ has some captions for the pictures.	The storyboard: ☐ has two pictures showing events in Maya Lin's life. ☐ has few captions for the pictures.

Project Score: _____

The Life of Daniel Boone

Consider students' reading and comprehension levels and assign the appropriate Reader.

▶ Approaching Level
- GR: G
- Benchmark: 14
- Lexile Level: 320

▶ On Level
- GR: L
- Benchmark: 24
- Lexile Level: 650

▶ Beyond Level
- GR: O
- Benchmark: 34
- Lexile Level: 700

Summary

Children read about the life of Daniel Boone and his work in the building of a road across the mountains so people could move to and settle in the west.

Objectives

- Apply unit reading strategies and skills.
- Learn about the life of Daniel Boone.

Activate Prior Knowledge

- Ask children to preview the reader's cover, table of contents, and illustrations to make predictions about the events in the story. Ask: **How do people settle in a new place? Why would people need to build a fort on the frontier? How can a fort help people be safe during conflicts?**

GO Vocabulary!

Write the common vocabulary words (*conflicts*, *fort*, and *settle*) on the board. Have volunteers predict the meanings of the words. As a class, create definitions for each word. Ask: **Based on the words, what do you think this story is about?**

networks

Go to connected.mcgraw-hill.com for additional resources:
- Leveled Reader Database
- Leveled Reader Answer Key

Active Teaching

Remind children that when they compare and contrast, they think about how things are alike and different. Write the following questions on the board.

Develop Comprehension

Ask:

1. *How was Daniel Boone's boyhood like that of many boys today? How was it different?* **L2**
2. *What important things did Daniel Boone do?* **L1**
3. *How was life different in Daniel's time than it is today?* **L2**

Leveled Reader Project

Name _____ Date _____

Use the book, *The Life of Daniel Boone,* and what you've learned about frontier life to make a picture book showing events in Daniel Boone's life. Make sure to draw pictures for each event from the story. Include captions for your illustrations.

Picture Book Rubric

4 Exemplary	3 Accomplished	2 Developing	1 Beginning
The picture book:	**The picture book:**	**The picture book:**	**The picture book:**
☐ has pictures for more than three events.	☐ has pictures for three events.	☐ has pictures for two events.	☐ has a picture for one event.
☐ has captions for all the pictures.	☐ has captions for several pictures.	☐ has captions for some pictures.	☐ has a caption for the picture.
☐ has few errors in capitalization and spelling.	☐ has some errors in capitalization and spelling.	☐ has several errors in capitalization and spelling.	☐ has serious errors in capitalization and spelling.

Project Score: _____

The Supreme Court

Consider students' reading and comprehension levels and assign the appropriate Reader.

▶ Approaching Level
- GR: M
- Benchmark: 28
- Lexile Level: 320

▶ On Level
- GR: M
- Benchmark: 28
- Lexile Level: 650

▶ Beyond Level
- GR: O
- Benchmark: 34
- Lexile Level: 700

Summary

Children read about the Supreme Court—what is does, how the justices are chosen, when it meets, and how long there has been a Supreme Court.

Objectives

- Apply unit reading strategies and skills.
- Learn about what the Supreme Court justices do.

Activate Prior Knowledge

- Ask children to preview the reader's cover, table of contents, illustrations, and first two sections of text to make predictions about what they will learn in the book. Ask: **"What does the Supreme Court do?"**

GO Vocabulary!

On the board, write the following vocabulary words from the reader. (*cases, justices, law, opinions*) Have children predict the meanings of each word. Then help them check the glossary and correct their meanings as needed. Explain that *justice* is the name for a person on the Supreme Court. Have children find pictures of the justices in the book. Then discuss laws and how justices make sure laws are fair.

networks

Go to connected.mcgraw-hill.com for additional resources:
- Leveled Reader Database
- Leveled Reader Answer Key

Active Teaching

Remind children that a cause is person, thing, or event that makes something happen. An effect is what happens. Write the following questions on the board.

Develop Comprehension

Ask:

1. *Why do we have a Supreme Court?* **L2**
2. *What happens in the Supreme Court?* **L1**
3. *Why are Supreme Court justices important people in our government?* **L2**

Leveled Reader Project

Name _____ Date _____

Have children review the information in the reader. Then ask them to write three cause and effect relationships in a graphic organizer. Invite volunteers to share one of their cause and effect relationships with the class.

Supreme Court Graphic Organizer

4 Exemplary	3 Accomplished	2 Developing	1 Beginning
The graphic organizer:	**The graphic organizer:**	**The graphic organizer:**	**The graphic organizer:**
☐ includes more than three cause and effect relationships.	☐ includes three cause and effect relationships.	☐ includes two cause and effect relationships.	☐ includes one cause and effect relationship.
The student:	**The student:**	**The student:**	**The student:**
☐ contributes constructively and creatively to the group.	☐ contributes to the group.	☐ somewhat contributes to the group.	☐ has difficulty contributing or contributes inappropriately to the group.

Project Score: _____

People Helping People: After Hurricane Katrina

Consider students' reading and comprehension levels and assign the appropriate Reader.

▶ Approaching Level
- GR: J
- Benchmark: 16
- Lexile Level: 210

▶ On Level
- GR: M
- Benchmark: 28
- Lexile Level: 380

▶ Beyond Level
- GR: O
- Benchmark: 34
- Lexile Level: 690

Summary

Students read about Hurricane Katrina and its aftereffects, including how people helped the victims recover from the storm.

Objectives

- Learn about how people helped others after Hurricane Katrina.
- Apply reading strategies and skills.

Activate Prior Knowledge

- Remind students that they have been learning about how people make positive contributions by volunteering to help others.
- Tell students that they are going to read a book about people helping other people recover from Hurricane Katrina.
- Ask students to tell you what they know about hurricanes. Then ask what they know about Hurricane Katrina.

GO Vocabulary!

Use the glossary in the back of each book to write the words common to all three levels on the board. Clarify the words through additional examples and sentences. Discuss how the words are connected to each other.

networks

Go to **connected.mcgraw-hill.com** for additional resources:
- Leveled Reader Database
- Leveled Reader Answer Key

Active Teaching

As students read, encourage them to think about how they would summarize the story.

Develop Comprehension

Ask:

1. *What states did Hurricane Katrina hit?* (Mississippi, Alabama, Louisiana) **L1**

2. **Summarize** *What kind of damage can a hurricane cause?* (destroy homes and injures people) **L2**

3. **Summarize** *How did people help others during Hurricane Katrina?* (people helped the survivors get food, water, and shelter) **L2**

Leveled Reader Project

Name _____   Date _____

Use the book, *People Helping People: After Hurricane Katrina,* and what you've learned about people being responsible citizens to write a newspaper article summarizing the efforts of people to help the survivors of Hurricane Katrina. Make sure to include details from the story in your article.

Newspaper Article Rubric

4 Exemplary	3 Accomplished	2 Developing	1 Beginning
The newspaper article:	**The newspaper article:**	**The newspaper article:**	**The newspaper article:**
☐ has more than three details.	☐ has three details.	☐ has two details.	☐ has one or two details.
☐ has accurate descriptions of events.	☐ has mostly accurate description of events.	☐ has some accurate description of events.	☐ has few accurate description of events.
☐ has few errors in capitalization and spelling.	☐ has some errors in capitalization and spelling.	☐ has several errors in capitalization and spelling.	☐ has serious errors in capitalization and spelling.

Project Score: _____

Leveled Readers

Biography

George Washington Carver
The Plant Doctor

Consider students' reading and comprehension levels and assign the appropriate Reader.

Approaching Level
- GR: I
- Benchmark: 16
- Lexile Level: 450

On Level
- GR: L
- Benchmark: 24
- Lexile Level: 680

Beyond Level
- GR: O
- Benchmark: 34
- Lexile Level: 790

Summary

Students read about the life of George Washington Carver, who revolutionized the way farmers planted crops and found hundreds of ways to use peanuts.

Objectives

- Learn about the life of George Washington Carver.
- Apply reading strategies and skills.

Activate Prior Knowledge

- Ask students to preview the reader's cover, table of contents, illustrations, and first two sections of text to make predictions about the events in the story.
- Tell students that George Washington Carver was a scientist and teacher. Explain to students that they will read about how George overcame many obstacles to achieve his dreams. Tell students that they will also learn how George made life better for other people.

GO Vocabulary!

Write the following words on the board:

agriculture   slavery

Discuss the meaning of each word. Have students list the kinds of foods that are grown through agriculture. Then have students tell what they know about slavery.

networks

Go to connected.mcgraw-hill.com for additional resources:
- Leveled Reader Database
- Leveled Reader Answer Key

Active Teaching

As students read, ask them to think about the sequence of events in George Washington Carver's life. Have pairs of students list important events in his life on a sequence graphic organizer.

Develop Comprehension

Ask:

1. *What happened in George Washington Carver's early life?* (George Washington Carver was born into slavery. He lost his mother at a young age.) **L2**

2. *What did George Washington Carver do to help farmers?* (George Washington Carver showed farmers how to make poor soil better. He told them to plant a different crop each year. George Washington Carver also found many new ways to use peanuts.) **L2**

3. **Sequence** *What is the order of events in George Washington Carver's education?* (George Washington Carver left home when he was 12 to attend high school in Kansas. Then he went to college in Iowa, where he studied agriculture.) **L2**

Leveled Reader Project

Name _____ Date _____

Create a time line of important events in George Washington Carver's life. Draw or glue pictures of George Washington Carver on your time line. Write captions about each picture.

Time Line of George Washington Carver's Life Rubric

4 Exemplary	3 Accomplished	2 Developing	1 Beginning
The time line:	**The time line:**	**The time line:**	**The time line:**
☐ has five or more pictures showing events in George's life.	☐ has four pictures showing events in George's life.	☐ has three pictures showing events in George's life.	☐ has two pictures showing events in George's life.
☐ has captions for each picture.	☐ has captions for each picture.	☐ has captions for each picture.	☐ has captions for each picture.
☐ has no errors in capitalization, punctuation, and spelling.	☐ has few errors in capitalization, punctuation, and spelling.	☐ has some errors in capitalization, punctuation, and spelling.	☐ has many errors in capitalization, punctuation, and spelling.

Project Score: _____

Carl B. Stokes

Consider students' reading and comprehension levels and assign the appropriate Reader.

▶ Approaching Level
- GR: J
- Benchmark: 16
- Lexile Level: 390

▶ On Level
- GR: M
- Benchmark: 28
- Lexile Level: 460

▶ Beyond Level
- GR: O
- Benchmark: 34
- Lexile Level: 650

Summary

Students read about the life of Carl B. Stokes, the first African American mayor of a major United States city, and later a judge and United States ambassador.

Objectives

- Learn about the life of Carl B. Stokes.
- Apply reading strategies and skills.

Activate Prior Knowledge

- Ask students who the mayor of their town is and what the mayor does.
- Have students preview the reader's cover and table of contents to make predictions about the book.
- Then have students look at the pictures and read the captions to see if their predictions were correct.

GO Vocabulary!

Write the following words on the board:

ambassador   law   mayor   politics

Say the words aloud and have the students repeat them after you. Have pairs of students read the definitions for each word in the glossary of their readers. Regroup and discuss how the words are connected to each other.

networks
Go to connected.mcgraw-hill.com for additional resources:
- Leveled Reader Database
- Leveled Reader Answer Key

Active Teaching

As students read, ask them to pay attention to the causes and effects of events in Carl B. Stoke's life. Tell students that an effect is something that happens, and a cause is the reason it happened.

Develop Comprehension

Ask:

1. *Why did Carl believe that school was important?* (Carl's mother taught him about the importance of education.) **L2**

2. *What is the first office that Carl B. Stokes held?* (Carl was elected to the Ohio House of Representatives.) **L2**

3. **Cause and Effect** *What kinds of problems did Cleveland have when Carl became mayor, and what did he do to help the city?* (Cleveland had pollution, poverty, and riots. Mayor Stokes worked hard to fix the problems. He also tried to improve Cleveland's schools and housing.) **L2**

Leveled Reader Project

Name _____ Date _____

Write a report about Carl B. Stokes. Write Carl B. Stokes' name on the cover of your report and draw or glue a picture of him. On the next page, write a paragraph about Carl's life and contributions.

Report about Carl B. Stokes's Life Rubric

4 Exemplary	3 Accomplished	2 Developing	1 Beginning
The report:	The report:	The report:	The report:
☐ has Carl B. Stokes' name and picture on the cover.	☐ has Carl B. Stokes' name and picture on the cover.	☐ has Carl B. Stokes' name and picture on the cover.	☐ has Carl B. Stokes' name and picture on the cover.
☐ has five sentences describing Carl's contributions.	☐ has four sentences describing Carl's contributions.	☐ has three sentences describing Carl's contributions.	☐ has one or two sentences describing Carl's contributions.
☐ has no errors in capitalization, punctuation, and spelling.	☐ has few errors in capitalization, punctuation, and spelling.	☐ has some errors in capitalization, punctuation, and spelling.	☐ has many errors in capitalization, punctuation, and spelling.

Project Score: _____

From the Farm

Consider students' reading and comprehension levels and assign the appropriate Reader.

▶ Approaching Level
- GR: J
- Benchmark: 16
- Lexile Level: 320

▶ On Level
- GR: M
- Benchmark: 28
- Lexile Level: 480

▶ Beyond Level
- GR: P
- Benchmark: 38
- Lexile Level: 730

Summary

Students learn about a day in the lives of a farmer and the workers at a farm stand and a farmers' market.

Objectives

- Learn about what farmers do to sell their produce.
- Apply reading strategies and skills.

Activate Prior Knowledge

- Remind students that they have been learning about goods and services and meeting consumers' needs. Ask students to think about how these concepts apply to farming.
- Tell students that they are going to read a book about farming. They will learn about the fruits and vegetables farmers grow and how they sell them.
- Ask students to tell what they know about farming. Ask students to explain why farmers are important.

GO Vocabulary!

Write the following vocabulary words on the board:.

nutrients   produce

Discuss the meaning of each word. Have students look in the book to find examples of produce that farmers sell. Then ask students to think of other words related to farms and farming. Create a word web of these words on the board.

networks
Go to connected.mcgraw-hill.com for additional resources:
- Leveled Reader Database
- Leveled Reader Answer Key

Active Teaching

As students read, encourage them to think about the order that things happen in the story.

Develop Comprehension

Ask:

1. *What is the first thing a farmer does to get ready for market day?* (pick crops) **L1**

2. **Sequence** *What does a farmer do in order to sell the crops?* (wash the crops) **L2**

3. **Sequence** *What do farmers do at the farmers' market?* (sell their crops) **L2**

Leveled Reader Project

Name _____ Date _____

Use the book, *From the Farm*, and what you've learned about a farmer's day to create a sequence graphic organizer with all of the events mentioned in the story. The events should be listed in sequential order, from first to last.

Sequence Graphic Organizer Rubric

4 Exemplary	3 Accomplished	2 Developing	1 Beginning
The graphic organizer:	**The graphic organizer:**	**The graphic organizer:**	**The graphic organizer:**
☐ has six or more events.	☐ has five to six events.	☐ has four to five events.	☐ has at least three events.
☐ has accurate descriptions of events.	☐ has mostly accurate description of events.	☐ has some accurate description of events.	☐ has few accurate description of events.
☐ has few errors in capitalization and spelling.	☐ has some errors in capitalization and spelling.	☐ has several errors capitalization and spelling errors.	☐ has serious errors in capitalization and spelling.

Project Score: _____

Common Core State Standards

English Language Arts & Literacy in History/Social Studies, Science, and Technical Subjects

Reading Standards for Informational Text, Grade 2

Standards		Student Pages	Teacher Pages
Key Ideas and Details			
1.	Ask and answer such questions as *who, what, where, when, why,* and *how* to demonstrate understanding of key details in a text.	11, 121, 139, 145	10–11, 120–121, 138–139
2.	Identify the main topic of a multiparagraph text as well as the focus of specific paragraphs within the text.	4–5, 55	4–5
3.	Describe the connection between a series of historical events, scientific ideas or concepts, or steps in technical procedures in a text.	56, 62–63, 79, 128–129	56–57, 62–63, 78–79, 118–119, 128–129
Craft and Structure			
4.	Determine the meaning of words and phrases in a text relevant to a grade 2 topic or subject area.	6–8, 30–32, 64–66, 75, 92–94, 130–132	6–7, 30–31, 64–65, 74–75, 92–93, 130–131
5.	Know and use various text features (e.g., captions, bold print, subheadings, glossaries, indexes, electronic menus, icons) to locate key facts or information in a text efficiently.	23, 119	22–23
6.	Identify the main purpose of a text, including what the author wants to answer, explain, or describe.	90–91, 107	90–91, 106–107
Integration of Knowledge and Ideas			
7.	Explain how specific images (e.g., a diagram showing how a machine works) contribute to and clarify a text.	136–137	136–137
8.	Describe how reasons support specific points the author makes in a text.	90–91	90–91
9.	Compare and contrast the most important points presented by two texts on the same topic.	28–29, 41, 45, 49, 53	28–29, 40–41
10.	By the end of year, read and comprehend informational texts, including history/social studies, science, and technical texts, in the grades 2–3 text complexity band proficiently, with scaffolding as needed at the high end of the range.	*	*

* The McGraw-Hill networks™ program is designed to provide ample opportunity to practice the reading and comprehension of informational texts for history/social studies for grade 2. The use of this book will help students master this standard.

Teacher Notes

UNIT
1 Planner OUR WORLD

 **Maps help us understand the world.**

Student Portfolio

- *Show As You Go!*
  Use these pages to introduce the Big Idea. Students record information specific to each lesson. They use these pages to help them plan their Big Idea Project.

networks

- **Group Technology Project**
  Students use 21ˢᵗ century skills to complete a group extension activity of the unit project. Lesson plans, worksheets and rubrics are available online.

Student Portfolio

- **Big Idea Project**
  Students will work together to create a globe of their own. The Big Idea Project rubric is on page 25W.

Reading Skills

Student Portfolio

- **Reading Skill: Main Topic and Details**
  Pages 4–5. Common Core State Standards RI.2

networks

- **Skill Builders**
  Introduce and practice the reading skill.

Treasures Connection

Teach this unit with Treasures Unit 4, *A Way to Help Planet Earth*, pages 84–87.

Social Studies Skills

Student Portfolio

- **Primary Sources: Maps**
  Page 9

networks

- **Skill Builders**
  Introduce and teach analyzing primary and secondary sources.

Activity Cards

- **Center for Social Studies Skills Investigation**
  Use the center activity cards to help students explore Primary Sources, Geography, and Citizenship.

FOLDABLES®

Student Portfolio

- Students can create vocabulary Foldables right in their portfolios.

- Additional Foldables templates can be found on pages R2–R6 of your Teacher Edition. See page R1 for instructions.

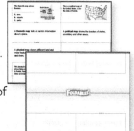

Assessment Solutions

- **McGraw-Hill networks™**
  Safe online testing features multiple question types that are easy to use and editable!

- **Self-Check Quizzes**

- **Worksheets**

UNIT 1 **At a Glance**

Lesson	Essential Question	Vocabulary	Digital Resources
1 Using Maps	**Why are maps important?**	thematic map map scale compass rose map key intermediate directions *element	Go to **connected.mcgraw-hill.com** for additional resources: • Interactive Whiteboard Lessons • Worksheets • Assessment • Lesson Plans • Content Library • Skill Builders • Videos • Use Standards Tracker on **networks** to track students' progress
2 Where We Live	**How do maps help us find places?**	political map physical map *travel	
3 Our Earth	**How do we find places on Earth?**	Equator Prime Meridian North Pole South Pole globe *imaginary	

*denotes academic vocabulary

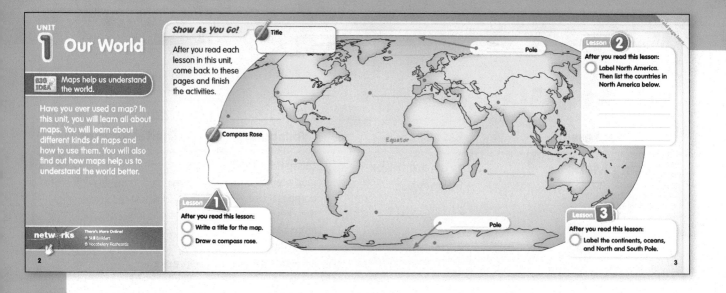

UNIT

1 Our World

BIG IDEA Maps help us understand the world.

Have you ever used a map? In this unit, you will learn all about maps. You will learn about different kinds of maps and how to use them. You will also find out how maps help us to understand the world better.

net**w**rks There's More Online!
• Skill Builders
• Vocabulary Flashcards

2

Show As You Go!

After you read each lesson in this unit, come back to these pages and finish the activities.

Title

Pole

Compass Rose

Equator

Pole

Lesson 1
After you read this lesson:
○ Write a title for the map.
○ Draw a compass rose.

Lesson 2
After you read this lesson:
○ Label North America. Then list the countries in North America below.

Lesson 3
After you read this lesson:
○ Label the continents, oceans, and North and South Pole.

3

Introduce the Unit

✓ Diagnostic Assessment

Display labeled maps of your school, neighborhood, and city around the classroom.

Ask: *Which of these maps would help us find our way around the school?*

Have students point to the appropriate map. Repeat this activity with questions about the other maps. Discuss how students would use each of these maps. For example, they may use the school map to find their way to the nurse's office.

Say: *In this unit, you will learn how to use many different kinds of maps. You will also learn how maps help us to bettter understand the world around us.*

Active Teaching

BIG IDEA Maps help us understand the world.
In this unit, students will learn how maps help us to better understand the world. Students will use the *Show As You Go!* pages throughout their study of this unit. As they read each lesson, students will use information from the lesson to complete these pages.

At this point, have students fold back the corner of this page. This will help them flip back to this page as needed. Explain to students that at the end of the unit, they will use the information collected on these pages to complete their Unit Project.

Differentiated Instruction

▶ **Approaching** Review the directions under each lesson head to help students identify what they should be looking for as they read. Have them circle the places and things they will need to find on the map. As lessons are completed, allow them to work in small groups to discuss and record the important details from the lesson.

▶ **Beyond** After students have read the directions under each lesson head, have them record one question they have about each lesson. As they read the lessons and record notes, encourage them to examine whether or not their question is answered. If it was not, challenge them to find the answer through outside research.

▶ **ELL** Review the directions under each lesson head and help to define unfamiliar words to make sure students understand what the note boxes are asking for. Have students work with a partner to complete each task.

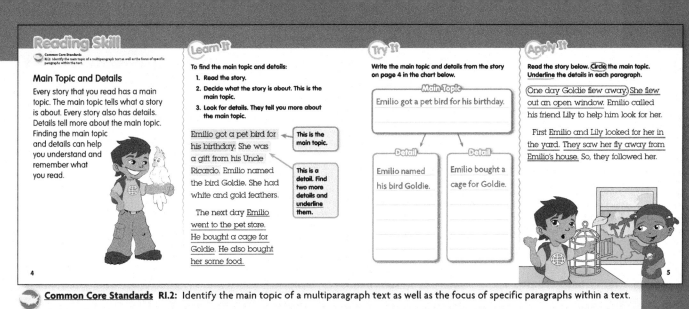

Main Topic and Details

Every story that you read has a main topic. The main topic tells what a story is about. Every story also has details. Details tell more about the main topic. Finding the main topic and details can help you understand and remember what you read.

Learn It

To find the main topic and details:

1. Read the story.
2. Decide what the story is about. This is the main topic.
3. Look for details. They tell you more about the main topic.

Emilio got a pet bird for his birthday. She was a gift from his Uncle Ricardo. Emilio named the bird Goldie. She had white and gold feathers.

The next day Emilio went to the pet store. He bought a cage for Goldie. He also bought her some food.

> This is the main topic.

> This is a detail. Find two more details and underline them.

Try It

Write the main topic and details from the story on page 4 in the chart below.

Main Topic

Emilio got a pet bird for his birthday.

Detail

Emilio named his bird Goldie.

Detail

Emilio bought a cage for Goldie.

Apply It

Read the story below. Circle the main topic. Underline the details in each paragraph.

One day Goldie flew away. She flew out an open window. Emilio called his friend Lily to help him look for her.

First Emilio and Lily looked for her in the yard. They saw her fly away from Emilio's house. So, they followed her.

4   5

Common Core Standards RI.2: Identify the main topic of a multiparagraph text as well as the focus of specific paragraphs within a text.

Active Teaching

(LEARN IT) Main Topic and Details

Say: *As I read, I think, "What is this story about?" Answering this question helps me to find the main topic of the story. Once I know the main topic of the story, I pay attention to sentences that tell me more information about the main topic. Those sentences are the details.*

(TRY IT) Encourage students to try the modeled strategy as they complete the TRY IT activity.

(APPLY IT) Have students complete the APPLY IT activity.

Ask:

1. *What question should you ask yourself to help find the main topic?* (What is this story about?) **L1**

2. *How can you tell which sentences in a story are the details?* (They are the sentences that tell you more information about the main topic.) **L2**

3. *Why is it important to identify the main idea and details of a story?* **L3**

Differentiated Instruction

▶ **Approaching** Review the LEARN IT activity as a small group. Do the TRY IT activity together. Have students complete the APPLY IT activity independently. Re-group to compare and correct.

▶ **Beyond** Have students write a short paragraph that includes a main topic and three details. Have them exchange paragraphs with a partner. Each student should identify the main idea and details of their partner's paragraph.

▶ **ELL** Have students discuss the images and predict what the passage might be about. Explain *details*. Read the passage one sentence at a time and have students identify the details. List students' responses. Read the list you have developed. Discuss what the responses have in common to identify the main idea.

netw☺rks

Go to connected.mcgraw-hill.com for additional resources:

- Skill Builder
- Graphic Organizer

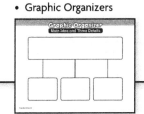

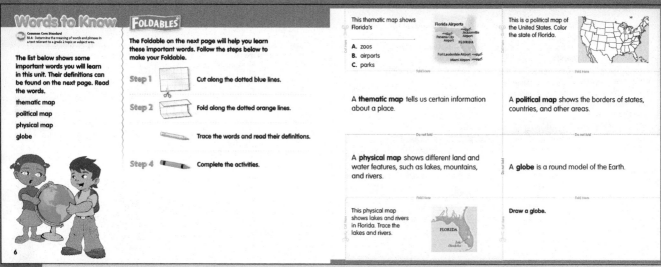

Words to Know **FOLDABLES**

Common Core Standard
RI.4: Determine the meaning of words and phrases in a text relevant to a grade 2 topic or subject area.

The list below shows some important words you will learn in this unit. Their definitions can be found on the next page. Read the words.

thematic map

political map

physical map

globe

The Foldable on the next page will help you learn these important words. Follow the steps below to make your Foldable.

Step 1   Cut along the dotted blue lines.

Step 2   Fold along the dotted orange lines.

          Trace the words and read their definitions.

Step 4   Complete the activities.

This thematic map shows Florida's _____

A. zoos
B. airports
C. parks

A **thematic map** tells us certain information about a place.

A **physical map** shows different land and water features, such as lakes, mountains, and rivers.

This physical map shows lakes and rivers in Florida. Trace the lakes and rivers.

This is a political map of the United States. Color the state of Florida.

A **political map** shows the borders of states, countries, and other areas.

A **globe** is a round model of the Earth.

Draw a globe.

Common Core Standards RI.4: Determine the meaning of unknown words and phrases in a text relevant to a grade 2 topic or subject area.

Words to Know

Active Teaching

FOLDABLES

1. Go to connected.mcgraw-hill.com for flashcards to introduce the unit vocabulary to students.

2. Read the words on the list on page 6 and have students repeat them after you.

3. Guide students as they complete steps 1 through 4 of the Foldable.

4. Have students use the Foldable to practice the vocabulary words independently or with a partner.

netw⚙rks

Go to connected.mcgraw-hill.com for additional resources:
• Vocabulary Flashcards
• Vocabulary Games
• Graphic Organizers

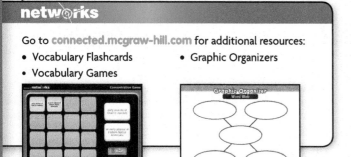

GO Vocabulary!
Use the graphic organizer below to help students gain a deeper understanding of each vocabulary word. Model for students how to complete the graphic organizer using the word *political map.* Have students complete the graphic organizer for the other words independently or with a partner.

Definition a map that shows the borders of states, countries, and other areas	**Description (in own words)** a map that shows lines or borders between places

WORD political map

Examples map of Florida map of the United States	**Non-Examples** map of airports map of rivers and lakes

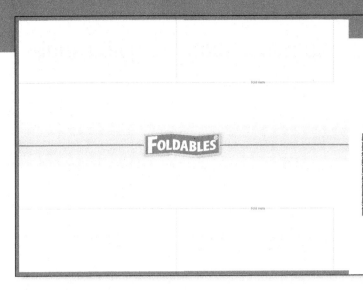

FOLDABLES

Primary sources are written or made by someone who saw an event happen. They teach us about people, places, and events.

Maps are one type of primary source. A map is a drawing of what a place looks like from above. We can learn about what people thought places looked like long ago by studying old maps. This map was created in 1662. That is more than 300 years ago!

networks
There's More Online!
• Skill Builders
• Resource Library

DBQ Document-Based Questions

Look at the map on this page. What does it show?

How is this map different from how a map looks today?

9

Differentiated Instruction

▶ **ELL** Write the vocabulary words from the Foldable on the board. Say each word aloud and have students repeat them. Next to each word, draw an example of it. Discuss each word with students.

WORD PLAY

Play Wordo to help students practice the unit vocabulary words.

• Print the Wordo card template from connected .mcgraw-hill.com. Make one copy per student and distribute to the class.

• Have students search the unit for vocabulary words, and write one word in each square.

• Orally present a sentence or definition for each word in the unit.

• Have students place counters or chips over the word that corresponds with the sentence or definition.

• A player wins when a vertical, horizontal, or diagonal line is covered.

When students are comfortable with the game, you may choose to have the students take turns calling the definitions and sentences.

Active Teaching

Use page 9 to teach your students about using primary source maps to learn about people, places, and events in the past. Explain to students that long ago, people did not know the shapes of our states or country. This map shows what people thought Florida looked like in 1662. Read the page together. Guide students through the written activities.

Ask: *What can we learn about life in the past from maps?* **L3**

networks

Go to connected.mcgraw-hill.com for additional resources:
• Skill Builders
• Resource Library

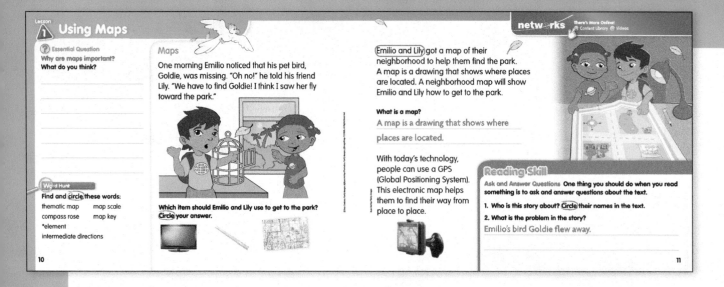

Lesson 1

Activate Prior Knowledge

Engage students' prior knowledge with a true/false activity. Read the following statements. Have each student hold their thumb up for true or their thumb down for false.

- *All places on Earth are close together.*
- *There is only one kind of map.*
- *Symbols on maps are decorations.*

Students responses will help identify their level of understanding.

⑦ Essential Question Why are maps important?

Have students explain what they understand about the Essential Question. Discuss their responses. Explain that everything they learn in this lesson will help them understand the Essential Question better. Remind them to think about how the Essential Question connects to the unit Big Idea: Maps help us understand the world.

Clarify Misconceptions

Students may think there is only one kind of map. Explain that there are many different types of maps and that each type has a different purpose.

Ask: *What are all of the things you would want a map to show? How could one type of map show all of this information?*

Active Teaching

Words To Know In each lesson, students will be learning both content and academic vocabulary. Academic vocabulary words are marked with an asterisk (*) on the lesson opener and are boldface within the text.

Have students find the words that are listed in the Word Hunt and read the definitions. Define the word *element*. Ask students to name different elements in the classroom.

Develop Comprehension

Read and discuss the pages together. Guide students through the written activities.

Ask:

1. *How will a map help Emilio and Lily find Goldie?* **L1**
2. *What information do you think will be on the neighborhood map?* **L2**

Differentiated Instruction

▶ **ELL** Have students describe what you might find in a neighborhood. Invite them to draw a picture of their neighborhood and write a sentence describing it.

Reading Skill

 Common Core Standard RI.1: Ask and answer such questions as *who, what, where, when, why,* and *how* to demonstrate understanding of key details in a text.

Ask and Answer Questions about Key Details

For additional practice, ask students to think of a question to ask a partner about the lesson. Have partners ask and answer each other's questions.

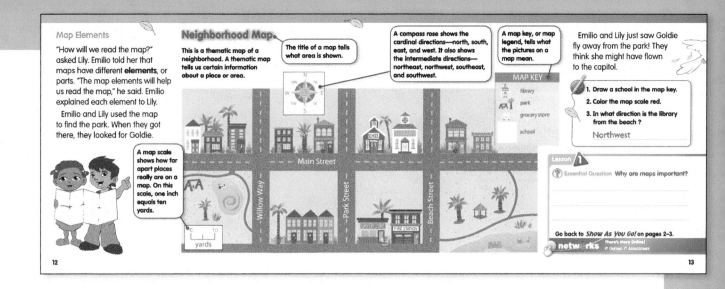

Map Elements

"How will we read the map?" asked Lily. Emilio told her that maps have different **elements**, or parts. "The map elements will help us read the map," he said. Emilio explained each element to Lily.

Emilio and Lily used the map to find the park. When they got there, they looked for Goldie.

A map scale shows how far apart places really are on a map. On this scale, one inch equals ten yards.

Neighborhood Map.

This is a thematic map of a neighborhood. A thematic map tells us certain information about a place or area.

The title of a map tells what area is shown.

A compass rose shows the cardinal directions—north, south, east, and west. It also shows the intermediate directions—northeast, northwest, southeast, and southwest.

A map key, or map legend, tells what the pictures on a map mean.

MAP KEY
library
park
grocery store
school

Emilio and Lily just saw Goldie fly away from the park! They think she might have flown to the capitol.

1. Draw a school in the map key.
2. Color the map scale red.
3. In what direction is the library from the beach ?

Northwest

Lesson 1

Essential Question Why are maps important?

Go back to *Show As You Go!* on pages 2–3.

networks There's More Online!
Games · Assessment

12

13

Active Teaching

Read the pages together. Guide students through the written activities. Discuss their responses.

Develop Comprehension

Ask:

1. *What is a map scale?* (Something that shows how far apart things actually are on a map.) **L1**

2. *What is a compass rose?* (Something that shows the cardinal and intermediate directions.) **L1**

3. *How do these elements help you find locations on a map?* **L3**

Summarize the lesson with the class. Then have students respond to the Essential Question. Discuss students' responses. Have students revisit their response on page 10 and compare it to their response at the end of the lesson. Discuss how their answers changed.

Show As You Go! Remind students to go back to complete the activities for this lesson.

Response to Intervention

(?) Essential Question **Why are maps important?**

If . . . students cannot give a response to the Essential Question, "Why are maps important?"

. . . .

Then . . . take students back to pages 10 through 13. Discuss why Emilio and Lily need to use a map and how they are using it.

Ask: *How will Emilio and Lily use their map?*

Following the discussion, allow students to respond to the Essential Question again.

networks

Go to connected.mcgraw-hill.com for additional resources:

• Interactive Whiteboard Lessons
• Worksheets

• Assessment
• Videos

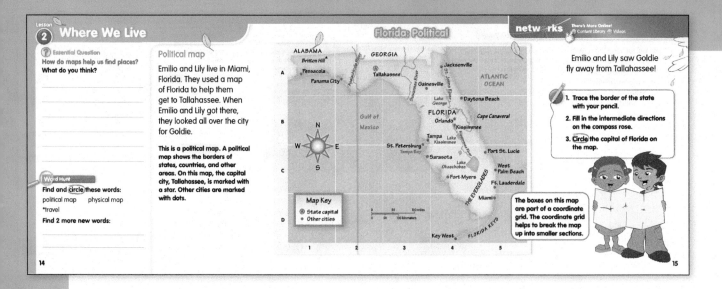

Lesson 2

Activate Prior Knowledge

Use masking tape to make a large 4 x 5 or 3 x 4 grid on the classroom floor.

Ask: *What kinds of places can we find in the neighborhood around our school?*

Examples are: houses, parks, stores, library, or swimming pool. As a class, make symbols for all of the places your class comes up with. Place the symbols on the grid in some similar fashion to where they are outside in the neighborhood. Next, put letter and number cards down along the edge of the grid. Have students give you the coordinates for each symbol.

? Essential Question How do maps help us find places?

Have students explain what they understand about the Essential Question. Discuss their responses. Explain that everything they learn in this lesson will help them understand the Essential Question better. Remind them to think about how the Essential Question connects to the unit Big Idea: Maps help us understand the world.

More About Coordinate Grids Places on Earth have addresses that tell their exact location. To describe the location of a place, geographers use maps with grids. A grid map is a map that is divided into squares. A letter and a number are used to name each square. The letters are on the side of the map. The numbers are on the top or bottom of the map. Drawing a grid over a map is a way to break a large map into small sections. Each section is the same size and shape. The grid makes it easy to find locations on the map.

Active Teaching

Words To Know Have students look through the lesson to find the words that are listed in the Word Hunt. Have them read the definitions of the content vocabulary words and use context clues or the glossary to determine the meaning of the academic vocabulary word *travel*. To help students understand the word *travel*, ask students about a time when they traveled to a faraway place.

Develop Comprehension

Read and discuss the pages together. Guide students through the written activities. Discuss their responses.

Ask:

1. *What is a political map?* (a map that shows the borders of states, countries, and other areas) **L1**
2. *What do the letters and numbers on a grid map do?* (break the map up into smaller sections) **L2**
3. *How does the grid make some maps easier to use?* **L3**

The United States

Emilio and Lily think Goldie flew north. "We need a map of the United States," Lily said. "It will help us **travel** north."

"Maybe she flew to our nation's capital, Washington, D.C.," Emilio said.

Emilio and Lily used a map of the United States to get to Washington, D.C. Once there, they looked all over for Goldie.

Washington, D.C.

The United States: Political

Emilio and Lily saw Goldie fly away from Washington, D.C.!

1. Find your state on the map and circle it.
2. Draw a box around Washington, D.C.

Active Teaching

Read pages 16 and 17 together. Guide students through the written activities.

Develop Comprehension

Ask:

1. *What type of map are Emilio and Lily using?* (a political map) **L1**
2. *What direction is Washington, D.C., from your hometown?* **L1**
3. *Why is Washington, D.C., indicated on a map with a star that is circled?* **L2**

DID YOU KNOW

Ask: *Did you know that D.C. stands for District of Columbia?*

Washington D.C. is the only city in our nation that is not part of any state. The capital lies within a segment of land that is administered by the federal government and called the District of Columbia.

☑ Formative Assessment

Have students summarize what they know about political maps. Have them draw a picture of a political map or write a brief description of one. Use this assessment to monitor student understanding and identify need for intervention.

Differentiated Instruction

▶ **Approaching** Have students identify their state and the surrounding states with a partner.

▶ **Beyond** Have students make a list or name aloud the 50 states in the United States.

▶ **ELL** Have students point to and name Washington, D.C. Discuss together what Washington, D.C., is and how it is shown on a map.

netw⊙rks

Go to connected.mcgraw-hill.com for additional resources:

- Interactive Whiteboard Lessons
- Assessment
- Worksheets

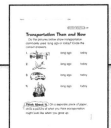

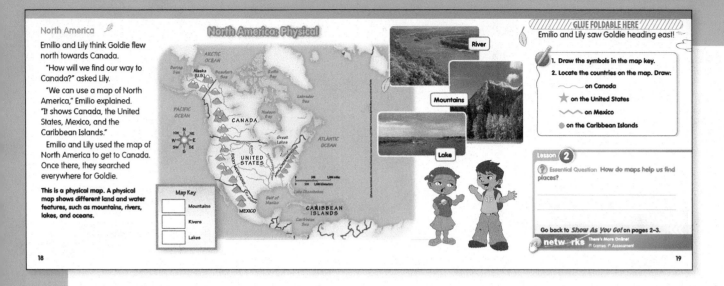

Lesson 2

Active Teaching

Read pages 18 and 19 together. Guide students through the written activities.

Develop Comprehension

Ask:

1. *What is a physical map?* (a map that shows different land and water features) **L1**

2. *What countries are in North America?* (Canada, the United States, Mexico, and the Caribbean Islands) **L1**

3. *How is a political map different from a physical map?* (One shows borders, and the other shows land and water features.) **L3**

Summarize the lesson with the class. Then have students respond to the Essential Question. Discuss students' responses. Have students revisit their response on page 14 and compare it to their response at the end of the lesson. Discuss how their answers changed.

> ***Show As You Go!*** Remind students to go back to complete the activities for this lesson.

Page Power

FOLDABLES® Interact more with the page. Have students create a Notebook Foldable to assist them in developing their understanding of map elements.

1. Provide each student with a copy of Foldable 1A from the Notebook Foldables section at the back of this book.

2. Have students construct the Foldable and glue its anchor tab on the top right corner of page 19.

3. On the Foldable flap, have students write the names of different land and water features that found near their home and school.

4. Under the flaps, have students draw an example of each feature.

Response to Intervention

? Essential Question How do maps help us find places?

If . . . students cannot give a substantiated response to the Essential Question, "How do maps help us find places?"
. . . .

Then . . . take students back to pages 14 through 19. Discuss how Emilio and Lily used their maps and the places they went.

Ask: *What places did Emilio and Lily go to in order to find Goldie?*

Following the discussion, allow students to respond to the Essential Question again.

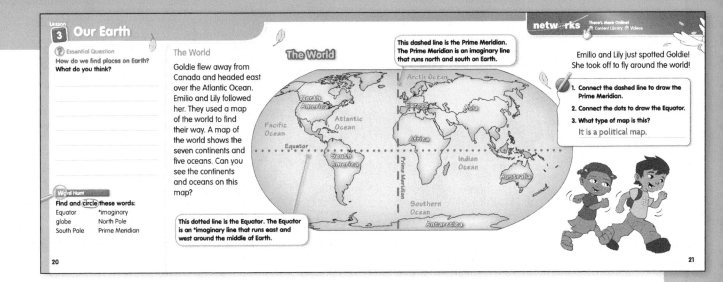

Activate Prior Knowledge

Engage students in a discussion about the shape of Earth. Show a globe and discuss how it is a model of Earth.

Ask: *Why do you think people don't usually carry around globes? What would the problems be with carrying a globe around?*

Some answers might include it is too big or not detailed enough. Bring up maps. Lead a discussion about how a map is not a true model of Earth. In front of the class or in small groups, peel an orange and try to lay the peel out as one smooth, flat piece. A tangerine sometimes peels best this way. Then discuss how, just like a map, the curved skin can't be made to lay flat.

Ask: *How did map makers solve this problem?*
Discuss as a class and come up with ideas while you fill in the real ways maps are distorted to show things.

(?) Essential Question How do we find places on Earth?
Have students explain what they understand about the Essential Question. Discuss their responses. Explain that everything they learn in this lesson will help them understand the Essential Question better. Remind them to think about how the Essential Question connects to the unit Big Idea: Maps help us understand our world.

Active Teaching

Words To Know Have students look through the lesson to find the words that are listed in the Word Hunt. Have them read the definitions of the content vocabulary words and use context clues or the glossary to determine the meaning of the academic vocabulary word *imaginary*. To help students understand the word *imaginary,* have them describe several things that are not real.

Develop Comprehension
Read and discuss the pages together. Guide students through the written activities. Discuss their responses.

Ask:

1. *What is the Equator?* (an imaginary line that runs east and west around the middle of Earth) **L1**

2. *What is the Prime Meridian?* (an imaginary line that runs north and south around Earth) **L1**

3. *How do the Equator and Prime Meridian help us find places?* **L3**

Differentiated Instruction

▶ **ELL** Have students look at the map on pages 20–21. Point to the Equator and Prime Meridian and say the names aloud with your students. Discuss what the Equator and Prime Meridian are.

Globes

Emilio and Lily then used a **globe** to see where Goldie might have flown. A globe is a round model of the Earth. You can spin a globe to see each part of Earth.

////// GLUE FOLDABLE HERE //////

1. Draw lines for the Equator and Prime Meridian on the globe.
2. Why would you use a globe instead of a map?

The very top of the Earth is called the North Pole.

The very bottom of the Earth is called the South Pole.

Emilio and Lily finally found Goldie on the continent of Asia. They were so happy to find her! They used all of their maps to help them get back home. When they got there, they thought about how maps helped them find places on Earth and bring Goldie back home!

Reading Skill
Know and Use text Features Certain text features can help you locate information quickly.

What text features on these pages help you find key words quickly?

The bold print and yellow color help

you find key words quickly.

Lesson 3
? Essential Question How do we find places on Earth?

Go back to *Show As You Go!* on pages 2–3.

net works   There's More Online!
◉ Games ◉ Assessment

Lesson 3

Active Teaching

Read pages 22 and 23 together. Guide students through the written activities.

Develop Comprehension

Ask:

1. *What is a globe?* (a model of Earth) **L1**
2. *How are globes different from maps?* **L2**
3. *How did maps help Emilio and Lily find Goldie?* **L3**

Summarize the lesson with the class. Then have students respond to the Essential Question. Discuss students' responses. Have students revisit their response on page 20 and compare it to their response at the end of the lesson. Discuss how their answers changed.

> ***Show As You Go!*** Remind students to go back to complete the project on the Unit Opener.

Reading Skill

Common Core Standard RI.5: Know and use various text features (e.g., captions, bold print, subheadings, glossaries, indexes, electronic menus, icons) to locate key facts or information in a text efficiently.

Know and Use Text Features For additional practice, ask students to look up the lesson's highlighted words in the glossary.

Ask: *Why is the glossary a useful text feature?*
Guide students to the conclusion that the glossary provides quick access to the definitions of key words.

Response to Intervention

? **Essential Question How do we find places on Earth?**

If . . . students cannot give a response to the Essential Question, "How do we find places on Earth?"

. . . .

Then . . . take students back to pages 20 through 23. Discuss how Emilio and Lily found the places they needed to go in order to find Goldie.

Ask: *How did Emilio and Lily find Goldie?*

Following the discussion, allow students to respond to the Essential Question again.

Page Power

FOLDABLES Interact more with the page. Have students create a Notebook Foldable to assist them in developing their understanding of maps and globes.

1. Provide students with a copy of Foldable 1B from the Notebook Foldables section at the back of this book.

2. Have students construct the Foldable and glue its anchor tab where indicated on page 22.

3. On the Foldable flaps, have students write the words *map* and *globe*.

4. On the backs of the flaps, have students draw or glue a picture of each. Have students write a sentence about each concept.

net works

Go to **connected.mcgraw-hill.com** for additional resources:

- Interactive Whiteboard Lessons
- Worksheets
- Assessment
- Lesson Plans

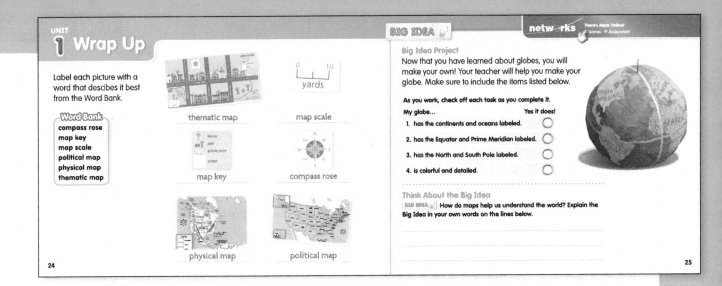

Label each picture with a word that descibes it best from the Word Bank.

Word Bank
compass rose
map key
map scale
political map
physical map
thematic map

thematic map

map scale

map key

compass rose

physical map

political map

BIG IDEA

netw⊙rks   There's More Online!
Games · Assessment

Big Idea Project
Now that you have learned about globes, you will make your own! Your teacher will help you make your globe. Make sure to include the items listed below.

As you work, check off each task as you complete it.

My globe...   Yes it does!

1. has the continents and oceans labeled.   ◯

2. has the Equator and Prime Meridian labeled. ◯

3. has the North and South Pole labeled.   ◯

4. is colorful and detailed.   ◯

Think About the Big Idea
BIG IDEA 💡 How do maps help us understand the world? Explain the Big Idea in your own words on the lines below.

Unit 1 Wrap Up

Word Match

Have students look at the pictures. Then have them choose a word from the Word Bank to label the pictures.

BIG IDEA 💡 **Unit Project**

Students will be making a papier-mâché globe to show what they learned in Unit 1.

- Read the checklist together and answer questions students may have about the project.

- Mix a paste of flour and glue.

- Have students cover a round balloon with strips of newspaper dipped in the paste.

- When the paste dries, have students draw, paint, and label the continents and oceans. (You can also print world outline maps from connected.mcgraw-hill.com and pass them out to students. Students can then cut, color, label, and glue the continents onto their globe.)

- Hang the globes in the classroom.

- Encourage self-reflection by asking:
  - What did you learn by doing this project?

- To assess the project, refer to the rubric on the following page.

netw⊙rks

Go to connected.mcgraw-hill.com for additional resources:

- Games
- Assessment
- Group Technology Projects

Differentiated Instruction

▶ **Approaching** Draw the oceans on the globes for students. Have students trace over the labels for the oceans with a black marker. Provide precut labels of the continents, North Pole, and South Pole for students. Have students use the classroom globe for reference as they paste the labels to their globes.

▶ **Beyond** Have students add additional details to their globes such as a compass rose, and labels for their hometown, the state and the national capitals, and the countries of North America.

▶ **ELL** Have students circle key words from the checklist that they need to include on their globes. Make sure students understand the directions for the project.

Response to Intervention

BIG IDEA 💡 Relationships affect choices.

If . . . students cannot give a substantiated response to the Big Idea, "Maps help us understand the world."

. . . .

Then . . . have students think about the maps that Emilio and Lily used. Ask students to describe how they used them. For example: How did Emilio and Lily get places? What elements on their maps helped them? Point out how maps helped them to find Goldie. Following the discussion, allow students to respond to the Big Idea again.

Name _____ Date _____

Model Globe Rubric

4 Exemplary	3 Accomplished	2 Developing	1 Beginning
The globe:	**The globe:**	**The globe:**	**The globe:**
☐ includes all continents and oceans	☐ includes most of the continents and oceans	☐ includes a few of the continents and oceans	☐ includes at least one continent and ocean
☐ contains accurate labels for the continents, oceans, Prime Meridian, Equator, and North and South Poles	☐ has mostly accurate labels for the continents, oceans, Prime Meridian, Equator, and North and South Poles	☐ has some accurate labels for the continents, oceans, Prime Meridian, Equator, and North and South Poles	☐ has few accurate labels for the continents, oceans, Prime Meridian, Equator, and North and South Poles
☐ includes correct colors to distinguish between land and water	☐ includes mostly accurate colors to distinguish between land and water	☐ includes some accurate colors to distinguish between land and water	☐ includes few accurate colors to distinguish between land and water
☐ contains few, if any, errors in the capitalization and spelling of the names of places	☐ contains some errors in the capitalization and spelling of the names of places	☐ contains several errors in the capitalization and spelling of the names of places	☐ contains serious errors in the capitalization and spelling of the names of places

Grading Comments: _____

_____

_____

_____

_____

_____

_____

_____

_____

Project Score: _____

Teacher Notes

UNIT
2 Planner NATIVE AMERICANS

 **BIG IDEA** Culture influences the way people live.

Student Portfolio

- *Show As You Go!*
  Use these pages to introduce the Big Idea. Students record information specific to each lesson. They use these pages to help them plan their Big Idea Project.

networks

- **Group Technology Project**
  Students use 21st century skills to complete a group extension activity of the unit project. Lesson plans, worksheets and rubrics are available online.

Student Portfolio

- Big Idea Project
  Students work together to create a museum display showcasing one of the Native American regions from the unit. The Big Idea Project rubric is on page 59W.

Reading Skills

Student Portfolio

- **Reading Skill: Compare and Contrast**
  Pages 28–29. Common Core State Standards RI.9

networks

- **Skill Builders**
  Introduce and practice the reading skill.

Leveled Readers

Use the leveled reader, *The Story of the Cherokee* (lesson plan on pages T16–T17) with Lesson 1 and *Maya Lin Artist and Architect*, (lesson plan on pages T18–T19) with Lesson 6.

Treasures Connection

Teach this unit with Treasures Unit 5, *Pushing Up the Sky*, pages 198–212.

Social Studies Skills

Student Portfolio

- **Primary Sources: Artifacts**
  Page 33

networks

- **Skill Builders**
  Introduce and teach analyzing primary and secondary sources.

Activity Cards

- **Center for Social Studies Skills Investigation**
  Use the center activity cards to help students explore Primary Sources, Geography, and Citizenship.

FOLDABLES

Student Portfolio

- Students can create vocabulary Foldables right in their portfolios.

- Additional Foldables templates can be found on pages R2–R6 of your Teacher Edition.

Assessment Solutions

- **McGraw-Hill networks™**
  Safe online testing features multiple question types that are easy to use and editable!

- **Self-Check Quizzes**

- **Worksheets**

UNIT 2 **At a Glance**

	Lesson	Essential Question	Vocabulary	Digital Resources
1	**Native Americans of the Southeast Woodlands**	How does where you live affect how you live?	region culture *belief	Go to **connected.mcgraw-hill.com** for additional resources:
2	**Native Americans of the Northeast Woodlands**	How did the land in the Northeast Woodlands affect the lives of Native Americans?	crop *gather	• Interactive Whiteboard Lessons
3	**Native Americans of the Plains**	How did the land shape the culture of Native Americans on the Plains?	prairie *herd	• Worksheets • Assessment
4	**Native Americans of the Southwest**	How did the desert affect the lives of Native Americans?	desert *level	• Lesson Plans • Content Library
5	**Native Americans of the Pacific Northwest**	How did the natural resources in the Pacific Northwest affect Native Americans?	natural resource *material	• Skill Builders • Videos
6	**Changing Communities**	What changes a community?	immigrant settlement *force	• Use Standards Tracker on **networks** to track students' progress

*denotes academic vocabulary

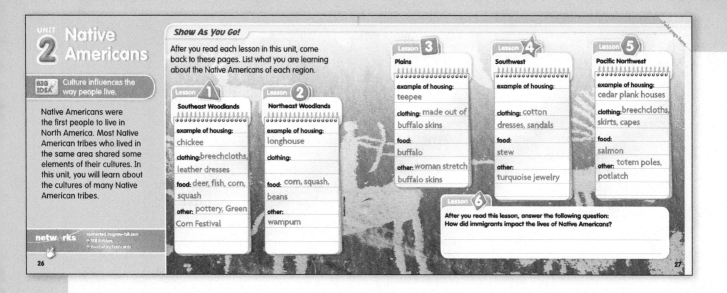

BIG IDEA Culture influences the way people live.

Native Americans were the first people to live in North America. Most Native American tribes who lived in the same area shared some elements of their cultures. In this unit, you will learn about the cultures of many Native American tribes.

networks
connected.mcgraw-hill.com
Skill Builders
Vocabulary Flashcards

Show As You Go!

After you read each lesson in this unit, come back to these pages. List what you are learning about the Native Americans of each region.

Lesson 1 Southeast Woodlands

example of housing: chickee

clothing: breechcloths, leather dresses

food: deer, fish, corn, squash

other: pottery, Green Corn Festival

Lesson 2 Northeast Woodlands

example of housing: longhouse

clothing:

food: corn, squash, beans

other: wampum

Lesson 3 Plains

example of housing: teepee

clothing: made out of buffalo skins

food: buffalo

other: woman stretch buffalo skins

Lesson 4 Southwest

example of housing:

clothing: cotton dresses, sandals

food: stew

other: turquoise jewelry

Lesson 5 Pacific Northwest

example of housing: cedar plank houses

clothing: breechcloths, skirts, capes

food: salmon

other: totem poles, potlatch

Lesson 6

After you read this lesson, answer the following question: How did immigrants impact the lives of Native Americans?

26

27

Introduce the Unit

✓ Diagnostic Assessment

Say: *In this unit, we will be learning about the cultures of various Native American tribes. Let's find out what you already know and what you would like to learn about Native Americans.*

Draw a KWL chart with the title *Native Americans* on chart paper. Have students fill out the K and W sections. Their responses will help identify their level of understanding.

Native Americans

What I **K**now	What I **W**ant to Learn	What I **L**earned

Say: *At the end of the unit, we will write what we learned in the last column of our chart.*

Active Teaching

BIG IDEA Culture influences the way people live.

In this unit, students will learn about the cultures Native American tribes shared in different parts of North America. They will also learn about the impact of immigrants on Native Americans. Students will use the **Show As You Go!** pages throughout their study of this unit. Students will use information from each lesson to complete the activities.

At this point, have students fold back the corner of page 27. This will help them flip back to this page as needed. Explain to students that at the end of the unit, they will use the information collected on these pages to complete the Big Idea Project.

Differentiated Instruction

▶ **Approaching** Review the directions with students and help define any unfamiliar words. After each lesson, allow students to work in a small group to complete the activity.

▶ **Beyond** Have students write sentences that compare the location, housing, clothing, food, or another element for two or more Native American cultures.

▶ **ELL** Read the headings on the chart with students. Define any unfamiliar words. As lessons are completed, allow students to work with a partner to discuss and record information on the pages.

Reading Skill

 Reading Skill

Common Core Standards
RI.9: Compare and contrast the most important points presented by two texts on the same topic.

Compare and Contrast

Things can be the same or different. We compare things to find out how they are the same. We contrast things to find out how they are different. Comparing and contrasting will help you understand what you read in social studies.

 Learn It

To compare and contrast:

1. Read the story about Scott and Nick.
2. Compare Scott and Nick by finding details that are the same.
3. Contrast Scott and Nick by finding details that are different.

Scott and Nick are pen pals. Both boys are in the second grade. Scott lives in South Carolina. He lives in a highrise apartment by the ocean. — *Details that are the same.*

Nick lives with his family on a farm in Nebraska. Nick can see barns and fields of corn from his house. — *Details that are different.*

Try It

Compare and contrast the story on page 28 in the chart below. Write the details that are the same in the middle. Write the details that are different in the outer part of each circle.

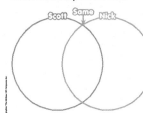

Scott   Same   Nick

Apply It

Read the story below. Circle details that are the same. Underline the details that are different.

(Scott and Nick are very busy boys.) (Both of them go to school in the) morning. Scott walks to school. Nick takes the bus. After school, (both boys go to soccer practice.) Scott likes to kick the ball. Nick likes to run. (On the weekends, Scott and Nick enjoy their free time.) Scott likes to swim. Nick likes to go horseback riding.

28   29

 Common Core Standards RI.9: Compare and contrast the most important points presented by two texts on the same topic.

Reading Skill

Active Teaching

LEARN IT Compare and Contrast

Read page 28 together to introduce comparing and contrasting. Then share this active reading strategy for comparing and contrasting two texts.

Say: *When I read two texts about the same thing, I pay attention to the important details in each text. Then I think about how the details are the same and different. This helps me focus on the important points from each text.*

Read LEARN IT together. Discuss how the boys in the story are the same and different.

TRY IT
Guide students as they complete the graphic organizer in the TRY IT activity.

APPLY IT
Have students complete the APPLY IT activity.

1. *What do the words* compare *and* contrast *mean?* **L1**
2. *What strategy will help you compare and contrast as you read?* (Pay attention to the details and look for things that are the same and different.) **L2**
3. *Why is it important to be able to compare and contrast?* **L3**

Write two short paragraphs about the same topic on the board. Have students compare and contrast the paragraphs. List their responses on a compare and contrast graphic organizer.

Differentiated Instruction

▶ **Approaching** Review the LEARN IT activity as a small group. Do the TRY IT activity together. Have students complete the APPLY IT activity independently. Regroup to compare and correct.

▶ **Beyond** Provide students with two paragraphs on the same topic. Have them complete a compare and contrast graphic organizer about the paragraphs.

▶ **ELL** Read the APPLY IT paragraph line-by-line with students. Discuss each detail.

Ask: *Whom does the detail describe? Does the detail tell how Scott and Nick are the same or different?*

Then have students write the details on the compare and contrast graphic organizer.

networks

Additional resources are found at connected.mcgraw-hill.com.
- Skill Builders
- Graphic Organizers

 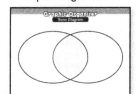

Unit 2 ▪ Reading Skill   **28–29**

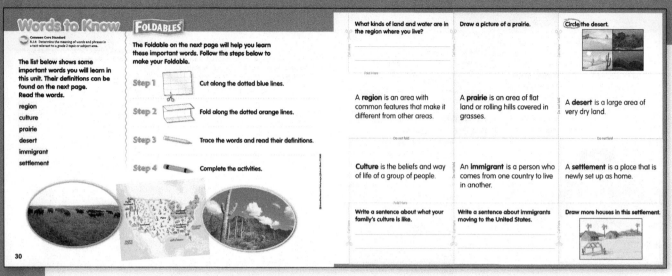

Common Core Standards RI.4: Determine the meaning of words and phrases in a text relevant to a grade 2 topic or subject area.

Words to Know
Active Teaching

FOLDABLES

1. Go to connected.mcgraw-hill.com for flashcards to introduce the unit vocabulary to students.

2. Read the words on the list on page 30 and have students repeat them after you.

3. Guide students as they complete steps 1 through 4 of the Foldable.

4. Have students use the Foldable to practice the vocabulary words independently or with a partner.

networks

Go to connected.mcgraw-hill.com for additional resources:

- Vocabulary Flashcards
- Vocabulary Games
- Graphic Organizers

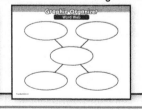

GO Vocabulary!

Use the graphic organizer below to help students practice the meanings of the words from the list. Model for students how to complete the graphic organizer using the word *region*. Then have students complete the graphic organizer for the other words independently or with a partner.

region

Definition	Description (in your own words)	Sentence or Picture
A region is an area with common features that make it different from other areas.	A region is a place with the same features that make it different from other places.	Our region of the United States has oceans, lakes, and swamps.

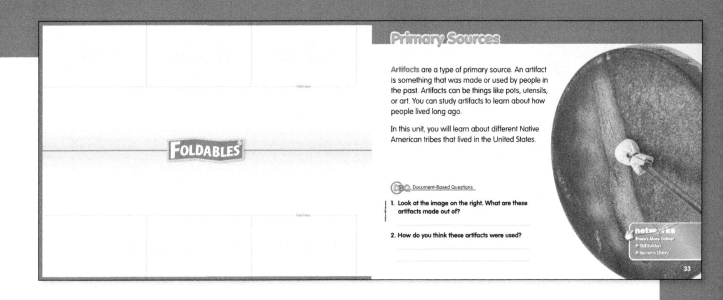

Primary Sources

Artifacts are a type of primary source. An artifact is something that was made or used by people in the past. Artifacts can be things like pots, utensils, or art. You can study artifacts to learn about how people lived long ago.

In this unit, you will learn about different Native American tribes that lived in the United States.

DBQ Document-Based Questions

1. Look at the image on the right. What are these artifacts made out of?

2. How do you think these artifacts were used?

networks
There's More Online!
• Skill Builder
• Resource Library

33

Differentiated Instruction

▶ ELL Have students draw pictures or write their own descriptions for each word on the list.

W O R D P L A Y

Play Concentration:

1. Have students write the words from the Foldable on one set of cards and the definitions on another set of cards.

2. Direct students to mix their cards and turn them face down.

3. To play the game, students need to match each word to its definition.

4. Students may play the game independently or with a partner.

Active Teaching

Read page 33 together. Discuss the meaning of the word *artifact*. Explain to students that the spoons in the picture were used by Seminole Native Americans. Have students describe the artifacts in the picture. Guide students through the written activities.

Ask:

1. *How are the spoons we use today the same and different from this artifact?* **L2**

2. *How do you think this artifact was made?* **L2**

3. *What does this artifact tell us about how people lived long ago?* **L3**

networks

Go to connected.mcgraw-hill.com for additional resources:

• Skill Builders   • Resource Library

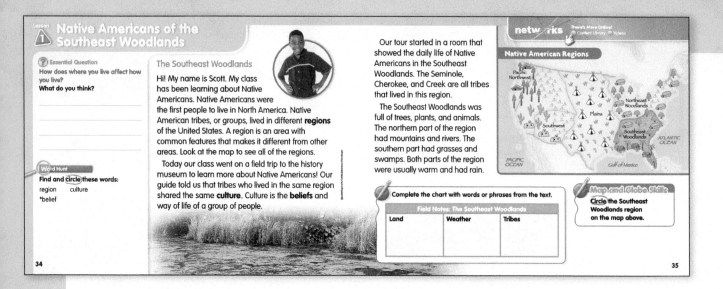

Activate Prior Knowledge

Explain to students that they will be reading a story about a boy named Scott who visits a history museum with his class to learn about Native Americans. Engage the students in a discussion about history museums.

Ask: *What kinds of things do you see in a history museum? What do you think we can we learn about Native Americans by visiting a history museum?*

Tell students that in this lesson, they will learn about Native Americans of the Southeast Woodlands region.

(?) Essential Question How does where you live affect how you live?

Have students explain what they understand about the Essential Question. Discuss their responses. Explain that everything they learn in this lesson will help them understand the Essential Question better. Remind them to think about how the Essential Question connects to the unit Big Idea: Culture influences the way people live.

Differentiated Instruction

▶ **ELL** Have students finish the following sentence frame with information from the pages: The Southeast Woodlands region had _____.

✔ Formative Assessment

Have students complete a concept map about Native Americans of the Southeast Woodlands region. Use this assessment to monitor students' understanding and identify need for intervention.

Active Teaching

Words To Know Have students look through the lesson to find the words that are listed in the Word Hunt. Then have them read the definitions of the content vocabulary words and use context clues or the glossary to determine the meaning of the academic vocabulary word *belief*. Explain that our beliefs may include how we think and feel about our surroundings. Tell students that our beliefs are a part of culture.

Develop Comprehension

Read pages 34 and 35 together. Have students study the map of Native American regions and find the Southeast Woodlands. Guide students through the written activities and discuss their responses to the Field Notes activity.

Ask:

1. *What are the names of Native American regions of the United States?* (Southeast Woodlands, Northeast Woodlands, Plains, Southwest, and Pacific Northwest) **L1**

2. *Where was the Southeast Woodlands region located?* (It was along the southeast coast of the United States.) **L1**

3. *How was the northern part different from the southern part of the Southeast Woodlands region?* (The northern part has mountains and rivers. The southern part had grasses and swamps.) **L2**

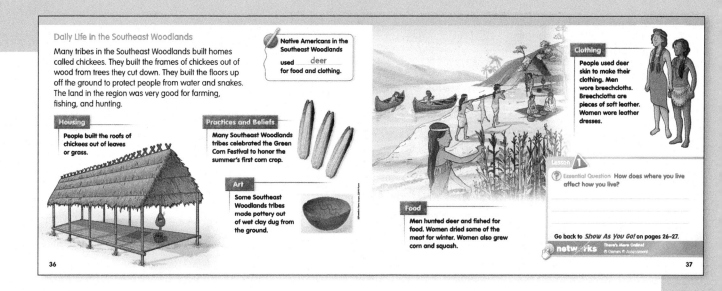

Daily Life in the Southeast Woodlands

Many tribes in the Southeast Woodlands built homes called chickees. They built the frames of chickees out of wood from trees they cut down. They built the floors up off the ground to protect people from water and snakes. The land in the region was very good for farming, fishing, and hunting.

Native Americans in the Southeast Woodlands

used ___deer___ for food and clothing.

Housing
People built the roofs of chickees out of leaves or grass.

Practices and Beliefs
Many Southeast Woodlands tribes celebrated the Green Corn Festival to honor the summer's first corn crop.

Art
Some Southeast Woodlands tribes made pottery out of wet clay dug from the ground.

Clothing
People used deer skin to make their clothing. Men wore breechcloths. Breechcloths are pieces of soft leather. Women wore leather dresses.

Food
Men hunted deer and fished for food. Women dried some of the meat for winter. Women also grew corn and squash.

Lesson 1

? Essential Question How does where you live affect how you live?

Go back to *Show As You Go!* on pages 26–27.

networks There's More Online! Games Assessment

36   37

Active Teaching

Tell students that the land affected the daily life of Native Americans of the Southeast Woodlands region. Explain that daily life includes:

- housing
- food
- clothing
- art, practices, and beliefs

Have students study the images on the pages. Read together. Have students discuss the pages with a partner. Then guide students through the written activities, except for the Essential Question.

Develop Comprehension

Ask:

1. *What were Chickees made out of?* (wood logs, leaves, and grass) **L1**

2. *How did Native Americans of the Southeast region use the land?* (They used the land for food, housing, and pottery.) **L2**

3. *Why do you think the Southeast Woodlands tribes had a celebration to honor corn?* **L3**

Use the leveled reader, *The Story of the Cherokee*, to extend and enrich students' understanding of the Cherokee. A lesson plan for this leveled reader can be found on pages T16–T17 at the front of this Teacher Edition.

Summarize the lesson with the class. Then have students respond to the Essential Question. Discuss their responses. Have students revisit their response on page 34 and compare it to their response at the end of the lesson. Discuss their answers.

> ***Show As You Go!*** Remind students to go back to the Unit Opener to complete the activities for this lesson.

Response to Intervention

? Essential Question **How does where you live affect how you live?**

If . . . students cannot give a substantiated response to the Essential Question, "How does where you live affect how you live?"

....

Then . . . engage students in a discussion about how the land affected life for Native Americans of the Southeast Woodlands region. Have them list specific examples from the text. List their responses on the board. Following the discussion, allow students to respond to the Essential Question again.

---

networks

Go to connected.mcgraw-hill.com for additional resources:

- Interactive Whiteboard Lessons
- Assessment
- Videos
- Worksheets

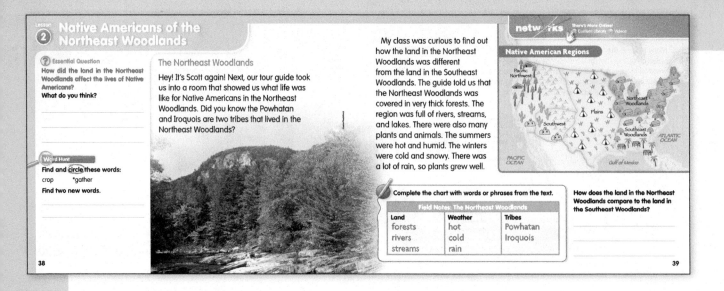

Lesson 2

Activate Prior Knowledge

Ask students to describe what they remember from the lesson about the land of the Southeast Woodlands. Have them explain how the land affected the daily life of Native Americans in that region. Tell students that in this lesson, they will learn about Native Americans of the Northeast Woodlands. Ask students to compare the two regions as they read the lesson.

? Essential Question **How did the land in the Northeast Woodlands affect the lives of Native Americans?**

Have students explain what they understand about the Essential Question. Discuss their responses. Explain that everything they learn in this lesson will help them understand the Essential Question better. Remind them to think about how the Essential Question connects to the unit Big Idea: Culture influences the way people live.

Differentiated Instruction

▶ **ELL** Have students draw a picture of crops growing in a garden and a person gathering the harvest. Ask them to use the words *crop* and *gather* in a sentence.

Map Skill and Globe Skill

For additional practice, have students locate the Northeast and Southeast Woodlands region on a classroom map.

Active Teaching

Words To Know Have students look through the lesson to find the words that are listed in the Word Hunt. Then have them read the definitions of the content vocabulary words and use context clues or the glossary to determine the meaning of the academic vocabulary words *crop* and *gather*. **Have students act like they are gathering crops from the garden.**

Develop Comprehension

Remind students to compare the how the Northeast Woodlands is the same and different from the Southeast Woodlands. Read and discuss the pages together. Guide students through the written activities. Discuss their responses on the Field Notes activity.

Ask:

1. *What direction are the Northeast Woodlands from the Southeast Woodlands?* (north) **L1**

2. *What was the land in the Northeast Woodlands like?* (It had thick forests, rivers, streams, and lakes.) **L2**

3. *How do you think Native Americans of the Northeast Woodlands used the land?* **L3**

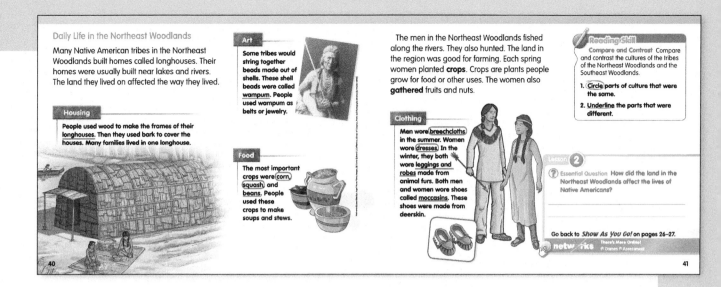

Daily Life in the Northeast Woodlands

Many Native American tribes in the Northeast Woodlands built homes called longhouses. Their homes were usually built near lakes and rivers. The land they lived on affected the way they lived.

Housing

People used wood to make the frames of their longhouses. Then they used bark to cover the houses. Many families lived in one longhouse.

Art

Some tribes would string together beads made out of shells. These shell beads were called wampum. People used wampum as belts or jewelry.

Food

The most important crops were corn, squash, and beans. People used these crops to make soups and stews.

The men in the Northeast Woodlands fished along the rivers. They also hunted. The land in the region was good for farming. Each spring women planted **crops**. Crops are plants people grow for food or other uses. The women also **gathered** fruits and nuts.

Clothing

Men wore breechcloths in the summer. Women wore dresses. In the winter, they both wore leggings and robes made from animal furs. Both men and women wore shoes called moccasins. These shoes were made from deerskin.

Reading Skill

Compare and Contrast Compare and contrast the cultures of the tribes of the Northeast Woodlands and the Southeast Woodlands.

1. Circle parts of culture that were the same.

2. Underline the parts that were different.

Lesson 2

Essential Question How did the land in the Northeast Woodlands affect the lives of Native Americans?

Go back to *Show As You Go!* on pages 26–27.

networks
There's More Online!
• Games • Assessment

Active Teaching

Have students study the images on pages 40 and 41. Then read and discuss the pages together. Ask students to describe how the houses, clothing, and food of the Northeast Woodlands were different from those of the Southeast Woodlands. Guide students through the written activities, except for the Essential Question.

Develop Comprehension

Ask:

1. *How did Native Americans of the Northeast Woodlands get their food?* (farming, hunting, fishing, and gathering) **L1**

2. *What did Native Americans of the Northeast Woodlands use to make their longhouses?* (They used wood from the land to make the frames. They covered the frames with strips of bark and mats made out of plants.) **L2**

3. *How do you think the weather affected the daily life of Native Americans of the Northeast Woodlands?* **L3**

Summarize the lesson with the class. Then have students respond to the Essential Question. Discuss their responses. Have students revisit their response on page 38 and compare it to their response at the end of the lesson. Discuss how their answers changed.

> ***Show As You Go!*** Remind students to go back to the Unit Opener to complete the activities for this lesson.

Reading Skill

Common Core Standards RI.9: Compare and contrast the most important points presented by two texts on the same topic.

Compare and Contrast Have students compare and contrast the information from this lesson with another text about the same topic.

Response to Intervention

(?) Essential Question **How did the land in the Northeast Woodlands affect the lives of Native Americans?**

If . . . students cannot give a substantiated response to the Essential Question, "How did the land in the Northeast Woodlands affect the lives of Native Americans?"

....

Then . . . reread the lesson with students. Discuss the housing, food, and clothing of Native Americans of the Northeast Woodlands.

Ask: *Why did the Native Americans of the Northeast Woodlands live in longhouses? Why did they eat corn, squash, and beans? Why did they wear clothing made of animal fur?*

Following the discussion, allow students to respond to the Essential Question again.

networks

Go to connected.mcgraw-hill.com for additional resources:

• Interactive Whiteboard Lessons
• Worksheet
• Assessment
• Videos

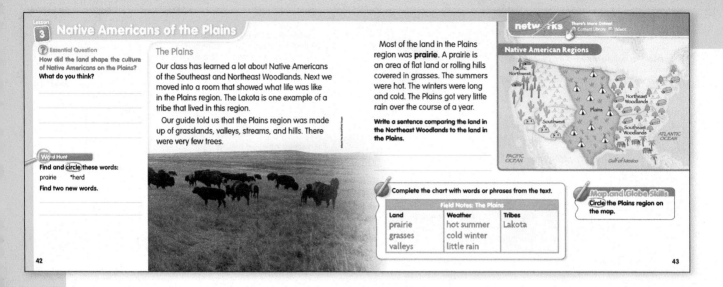

Lesson 3

Activate Prior Knowledge

Show students the Plains region on the classroom map. Have students close their eyes as you describe the land of the Plains region.

Say: *Imagine that you can see grassy hills and flat land for miles. You can see flowing streams and buffalo roaming the land. Unlike the Northeast Woodlands and Southeast Woodlands region, you see very few trees.*

Ask: *What do you think Native Americans of the Plains region used for food, clothing, and housing?*

Tell students that in this lesson, they will learn more about the daily life of Native Americans in the Plains region.

? Essential Question How did the land shape the culture of Native Americans on the Plains?

Have students explain what they understand about the Essential Question. Discuss their responses. Explain that everything they learn in this lesson will help them understand the Essential Question better. Remind them to think about how the Essential Question connects to the unit Big Idea: Culture influences the way people live.

Map Skill and Globe Skill

For additional practice, have students locate the Plains region on a classroom map.

Active Teaching

Words To Know Have students look through the lesson to find the words that are listed in the Word Hunt. Then have them read the definitions of the content vocabulary words and use context clues or the glossary to determine the meaning of the academic vocabulary word *herd*. Explain that herds of buffalo roamed the Plains region long ago. Ask students to think of other animals that move in herds. Explain that the buffalo were important to Native Americans of the Plains region.

Develop Comprehension

Read the pages together. Guide students through the written activities. Have them share their responses on the Field Notes activity.

Ask:

1. *What was the land in the Plains region like?* (It was made up of grasslands, valleys, streams, and hills.) **L1**

2. *How do you think Native Americans in the Plains region used the buffalo?* **L2**

3. *How is the Plains region different from the Northeast and Southeast Woodlands regions?* **L3**

Differentiated Instruction

▶ **ELL** Show students pictures of the following words: grasslands, valleys, streams, and hills. Point out the characteristics of each land feature in the pictures. Have students draw and label pictures of each land feature. Have them write the following title at the top of their paper: *Land in the Plains Region*. Then have students explain their pictures to a partner.

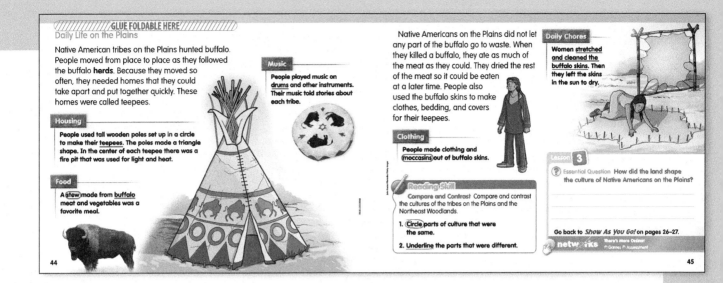

Daily Life on the Plains

Native American tribes on the Plains hunted buffalo. People moved from place to place as they followed the buffalo **herds**. Because they moved so often, they needed homes that they could take apart and put together quickly. These homes were called teepees.

Housing

People used tall wooden poles set up in a circle to make their teepees. The poles made a triangle shape. In the center of each teepee there was a fire pit that was used for light and heat.

Food

A stew made from buffalo meat and vegetables was a favorite meal.

Music

People played music on drums and other instruments. Their music told stories about each tribe.

Native Americans on the Plains did not let any part of the buffalo go to waste. When they killed a buffalo, they ate as much of the meat as they could. They dried the rest of the meat so it could be eaten at a later time. People also used the buffalo skins to make clothes, bedding, and covers for their teepees.

Clothing

People made clothing and moccasins out of buffalo skins.

Reading Skill

Compare and Contrast Compare and contrast the cultures of the tribes on the Plains and the Northeast Woodlands.

1. Circle parts of culture that were the same.
2. Underline the parts that were different.

Daily Chores

Women stretched and cleaned the buffalo skins. Then they left the skins in the sun to dry.

Lesson 3

Essential Question How did the land shape the culture of Native Americans on the Plains?

Go back to *Show As You Go!* on pages 26–27.

networks There's More Online!

Active Teaching

Have students look at the images on pages 44 and 45. Before they read, remind students to compare and contrast Native Americans of the Plains region with Native Americans of the Southeast Woodlands and Northeast Woodlands regions. Read the pages together. Guide students as they complete the written activities, except for the Essential Question.

Develop Comprehension

Ask:

1. *Why did Native Americans of the Plains region need homes that could be taken apart quickly?* **L2**

2. *Why were buffalo important to Native Americans of the Plains region?* **L2**

3. *What is the same about the cultures we have read about in Lessons 1 through 3? What is different?* **L3**

Summarize the lesson with the class. Then have students respond to the Essential Question. Discuss their responses. Have students revisit their response on page 42 and compare it to their response at the end of the lesson. Discuss how their answers changed.

> ***Show As You Go!*** Remind students to go back to the Unit Opener to complete the activities for this lesson.

Response to Intervention

? Essential Question How did the land shape the culture of Native Americans on the Plains?

If . . . students cannot give a substantiated response to the Essential Question, "How did the land shape the culture of Native Americans of the Plains?"

. . . .

Then . . . have students reread the lesson with an able partner.

Ask: *Why did Native Americans of the Plains live in teepees, not longhouses?*

Record students' responses on the board. Ask students to explain other ways that the land affected daily life for Native Americans of the Plains region. Following the discussion, allow students to respond to the Essential Question again.

Page Power

FOLDABLES Interact more with the page. Have students create a Foldable to assist them in comparing the housing of Native Americans from three regions.

1. Provide each student with a copy of Foldable 2A from Notebook Foldables section at the back of this book.

2. Have students construct the Foldable and glue its anchor tab at the top of page 44.

3. On the Foldable flaps, have students draw and label a longhouse and a chickee. Write the regions under the flaps.

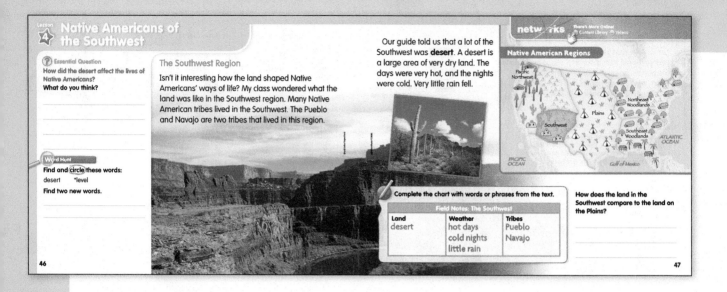

Lesson 4

Activate Prior Knowledge

Show students the Southwest region on the classroom map. Tell students that much of the land in the Southwest was desert. Ask students to tell what they know about deserts.

Say: *In this lesson, we will learn about the daily life of Native Americans in the deserts of the Southwest region of the United States.*

? Essential Question **How did the desert affect the lives of Native Americans?**

Have students explain what they understand about the Essential Question. Discuss their responses. Explain that everything they learn in this lesson will help them understand the Essential Question better. Remind them to think about how the Essential Question connects to the unit Big Idea: Culture influences the way people live.

netwrks

Go to **connected.mcgraw-hill.com** for additional resources:

- Interactive Whiteboard Lessons
- Worksheet
- Assessment

Active Teaching

Words To Know Have students find the word *desert* in the text and read the definition. Then, define the academic vocabulary word *level* for students.

Say: *Native Americans of the Southwest region lived in homes with many levels or floors.*

Ask: *How many levels are in your house or apartment?*

Develop Comprehension

Read the pages together. Have students turn to a partner and discuss the land of the Southwest. Guide students through the written activities. Discuss their responses on the Field Notes activity.

Ask:

1. *What was the weather like in the Southwest region?* (The days were very hot and dry. The nights were very cold.) **L1**

2. *How do you think the desert affected life for Native Americans in the Southwest region?* **L2**

3. *How is the land of the Southwest region different from the land in the Plains, Northeast Woodlands, and Southeast Woodlands?* **L3**

Differentiated Instruction

▶ **ELL** Show the students pictures of deserts of the Southwest. Then draw a circle with four quadrants. Write the title, "Desert," above the circle. Have students think of words to describe the deserts of the Southwest and write them in the four quadrants of the concept circle.

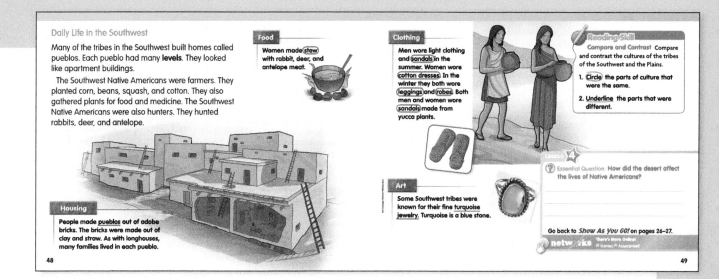

Daily Life in the Southwest

Many of the tribes in the Southwest built homes called pueblos. Each pueblo had many **levels**. They looked like apartment buildings.

The Southwest Native Americans were farmers. They planted corn, beans, squash, and cotton. They also gathered plants for food and medicine. The Southwest Native Americans were also hunters. They hunted rabbits, deer, and antelope.

Food
Women made stew with rabbit, deer, and antelope meat.

Housing
People made pueblos out of adobe bricks. The bricks were made out of clay and straw. As with longhouses, many families lived in each pueblo.

Clothing
Men wore light clothing and sandals in the summer. Women wore cotton dresses. In the winter they both wore leggings and robes. Both men and women wore sandals made from yucca plants.

Art
Some Southwest tribes were known for their fine turquoise jewelry. Turquoise is a blue stone.

Reading Skill
Compare and Contrast Compare and contrast the cultures of the tribes of the Southwest and the Plains.

1. Circle the parts of culture that were the same.

2. Underline the parts that were different.

Lesson 4

? Essential Question How did the desert affect the lives of Native Americans?

Go back to *Show As You Go!* on pages 26–27.

networks There's More Online!

48

49

Active Teaching

Have students study and discuss the images on pages 48 and 49. Before they read, remind students to compare and contrast Native Americans of the Southwest with the other tribes they learned about in previous lessons. Then read the pages together. Have students discuss the similarities and differences in small groups. Then guide students as they complete the written activities, except for the Essential Question. Discuss their responses.

Develop Comprehension

Ask:

1. *How did Native Americans of the Southwest region get their food?* (They were farmers and hunters.) **L1**

2. *How did Native Americans of the Southwest use the land?* **L2**

3. *Why did Native Americans in the Southwest live in pueblos, not chickees?* **L3**

Summarize the lesson with the class. Then have students respond to the Essential Question. Have students revisit their response on page 46 and compare it to their response at the end of the lesson. Discuss how their answers changed.

> ***Show As You Go!*** Remind students to go back to the Unit Opener to complete the activities for this lesson.

☑ Formative Assessment

Have students complete a concept map about Native Americans of the Southwest region. They should include descriptions of the housing, clothing, food, and art. Use this assessment to monitor students' understanding and identify the need for intervention.

Response to Intervention

? Essential Question **How did the desert affect the lives of Native Americans?**

If . . . students cannot give a substantiated response to the Essential Question, "How did the desert affect the lives of Native Americans?"

. . . .

Then . . . take students back through the lesson. Have students describe the housing, food, clothing, and art of Native Americans from the Southwest.

Ask: *Why was the housing, clothing, and art of Native Americans of the Southwest different from the other regions?*

Following the discussion, allow students to respond to the Essential Question again.

networks™

Go to connected.mcgraw-hill.com for additional resources:

• Interactive Whiteboard Lessons
• Worksheets
• Assessment

Transportation Then and Now
Do the pictures below show transportation commonly used long ago or today? Circle the correct answers.

1. long ago   today
2. long ago   today
3. long ago   today
4. long ago   today

Think About It On a separate piece of paper, draw a picture of what you think transportation might look like when you grow up.

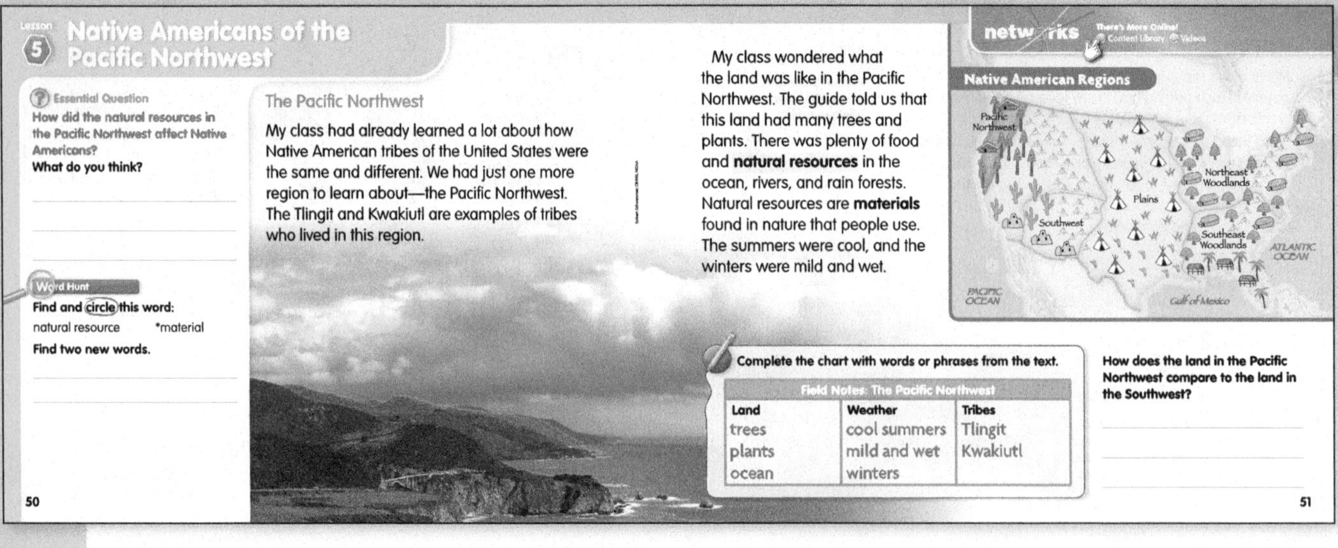
Lesson 5 Native Americans of the Pacific Northwest

Essential Question
How did the natural resources in the Pacific Northwest affect Native Americans?
What do you think?

Word Hunt
Find and circle this word:
natural resource *material
Find two new words.

The Pacific Northwest

My class had already learned a lot about how Native American tribes of the United States were the same and different. We had just one more region to learn about—the Pacific Northwest. The Tlingit and Kwakiutl are examples of tribes who lived in this region.

My class wondered what the land was like in the Pacific Northwest. The guide told us that this land had many trees and plants. There was plenty of food and **natural resources** in the ocean, rivers, and rain forests. Natural resources are **materials** found in nature that people use. The summers were cool, and the winters were mild and wet.

networks There's More Online! Content Library Videos

Native American Regions

Complete the chart with words or phrases from the text.

Field Notes: The Pacific Northwest		
Land	Weather	Tribes
trees plants ocean	cool summers mild and wet winters	Tlingit Kwakiutl

How does the land in the Pacific Northwest compare to the land in the Southwest?

50 51

Lesson 5

Activate Prior Knowledge

Show students the Pacific Northwest region on the classroom map.

Ask: *What body of water borders the Pacific Northwest on the west?*

Have students close their eyes and visualize as you describe the environment of the Pacific Northwest region.

Say: *Imagine that you live in the Pacific Northwest. You are surrounded by many cedar trees and plants. The front of your house faces the Pacific Ocean. There are rivers close to your house.*

Ask: *What do you think Native Americans used for food, clothing, and housing in the Pacific Northwest?*

Tell students that they will find the answer to that question in this lesson.

Essential Question How did the natural resources in the Pacific Northwest affect Native Americans?

Have students explain what they understand about the Essential Question. Discuss their responses. Explain that everything they learn in this lesson will help them understand the Essential Question better. Remind them to think about how the Essential Question connects to the unit Big Idea: Culture influences the way people live.

Active Teaching

Words To Know Have students look through the lesson to find the words that are listed in the Word Hunt. Then have them read the definitions of the content vocabulary words and use context clues or the glossary to determine the meaning of the academic vocabulary word *material*.

Say: *Water, trees, rocks, and soil are materials found in nature that are natural resources.*

Ask students to describe the uses of each of these resources.

Develop Comprehension

Read the pages together. Have students write the main points on a web titled, "Pacific Northwest." Guide students through the written activities. Discuss their responses on the Field Notes activity.

Ask:

1. *What kind of natural resources can be found in rivers?* (fish, water, and rocks) **L1**
2. *What other Native American regions had plenty of rain, trees, and rivers?* (the Southeast Woodlands and the Northeast Woodlands) **L1**
3. *How is the weather of the Pacific Northwest region different from the Southwest region?* **L3**

Differentiated Instruction

ELL Restate the definition of the word *natural resources*. Have students state the definition in their own words. Then show students pictures of the Pacific Northwest environment. Have them identify the natural resources in the pictures.

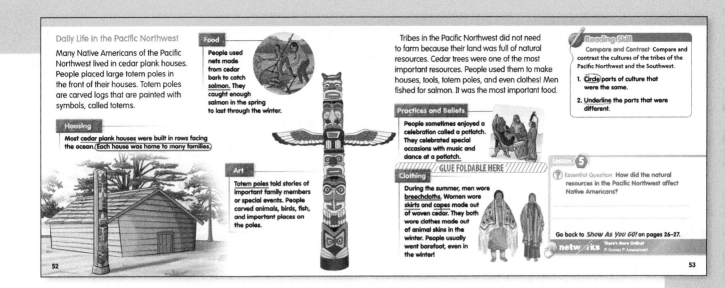

Daily Life in the Pacific Northwest

Many Native Americans of the Pacific Northwest lived in cedar plank houses. People placed large totem poles in the front of their houses. Totem poles are carved logs that are painted with symbols, called totems.

Food

People used nets made from cedar bark to catch salmon. They caught enough salmon in the spring to last through the winter.

Housing

Most cedar plank houses were built in rows facing the ocean. Each house was home to many families.

Art

Totem poles told stories of important family members or special events. People carved animals, birds, fish, and important places on the poles.

Tribes in the Pacific Northwest did not need to farm because their land was full of natural resources. Cedar trees were one of the most important resources. People used them to make houses, tools, totem poles, and even clothes! Men fished for salmon. It was the most important food.

Practices and Beliefs

People sometimes enjoyed a celebration called a potlatch. They celebrated special occasions with music and dance at a potlatch.

// GLUE FOLDABLE HERE //

Clothing

During the summer, men wore breechcloths. Women wore skirts and capes made out of woven cedar. They both wore clothes made out of animal skins in the winter. People usually went barefoot, even in the winter!

Reading Skill

Compare and Contrast Compare and contrast the cultures of the tribes of the Pacific Northwest and the Southwest.

1. Circle parts of culture that were the same.

2. Underline the parts that were different.

Lesson 5

Essential Question How did the natural resources in the Pacific Northwest affect Native Americans?

Go back to *Show As You Go!* on pages 26–27.

networks There's More Online! © Content © Assessment

Active Teaching

Have students study the images on the pages and share their observations. As they read, have students compare and contrast Native Americans from each region. Read the pages together. Then have partners discuss the similarities and differences between the Pacific Northwest and tribes from other regions. Next guide students as they complete the written activities, except for the Essential Question. Discuss their responses.

Develop Comprehension

Ask:

1. *Why were cedar trees an important natural resource for Native Americans of the Pacific Northwest?* (They used them to make houses, tools, baskets, nets for fishing, totem poles, and clothes.) **L1**

2. *What kind of clothing did Native Americans of the Pacific Northwest wear?* **L2**

3. *Why was salmon important to Native Americans of the Pacific Northwest?* (It was their main source of food.) **L3**

Summarize the lesson with the class. Then have students respond to the Essential Question. Discuss their responses. Have students revisit their response on page 50 and compare it to their response at the end of the lesson. Discuss how their answers changed.

Show As You Go! Remind students to go back to the Unit Opener to complete the activities for the lesson.

Response to Intervention

Essential Question How did the natural resources in the Pacific Northwest affect Native Americans?

If . . . students cannot give a substantiated response to the Essential Question, "How did the natural resources in the Pacific Northwest affect Native Americans?"

. . . .

Then . . . engage students in a discussion about the natural resources of the Pacific Northwest region. Have students describe how Native Americans from that region used the natural resources for housing, food, and clothing. List their responses on the board and read them together. Following the discussion, allow students to respond to the Essential Question again.

Page Power

FOLDABLES Interact more with the page. Have students create a Foldable to assist them in comparing the clothing of Native Americans from the Pacific Northwest and another region.

1. Provide each student with a copy of Foldable 2B from the Notebook Foldables section at the back of this book.

2. Have students construct the Foldable and glue its anchor tab above the picture of the clothing on page 53.

3. On the Foldable flap, have students draw or glue a picture of the clothing of another tribe. Name the region and describe the clothing.

4. Under the flap, tell how the clothing is the same or different.

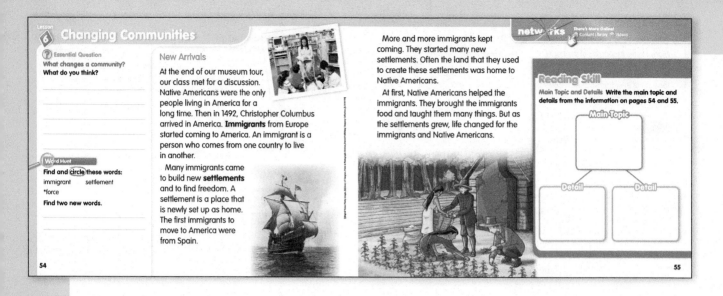

Lesson 6

Activate Prior Knowledge

Engage the students in role play to help them think about the impact of immigrants on Native Americans.

- Have a group of students play the roles of Native Americans in the Southeast Woodlands. Have them act out details from their daily life.

- Appoint different students to play the role of immigrants. Instruct them to make the students portraying Native Americans leave their homes.

Discuss the drama with the class. Encourage students to think about the perspectives of both the Native Americans and the immigrants.

Explain to students that in this lesson they will find out what happened to Native Americans when people from Europe moved to their land.

? Essential Question **What changes a community?**

Have students explain what they understand about the Essential Question. Discuss their responses. Explain that everything they learn in this lesson will help them understand the Essential Question better. Remind them to think about how the Essential Question connects to the unit Big Idea: Culture influences the way people live.

More About Immigrants and Native Americans In the early 1800s, many Native Americans in the Southeast lived peacefully with immigrants. Their right to their homeland had been guaranteed by treaties signed with the United States government. However, in 1830 Congress passed the Indian Removal Act. This act forced Native Americans to move to what Congress called the Indian Territory, which is now the state of Oklahoma.

Active Teaching

Words To Know Have students find the words in the text. Have them read the definitions for the words *immigrant* and *settlement*. Trace the route immigrants took across the Atlantic Ocean to get to America. Have students list the things immigrants would need in their new country.

Then define the academic vocabulary words *force* and *homeland*. Have students recall the role playing activity.

Say: *Native Americans were forced from their homelands by the immigrants.*

Paraphrase the sentence for students by saying that the immigrants made Native Americans leave their homes and their land.

Develop Comprehension

Read and discuss pages 54 and 55 together. Then have students list the reasons immigrants came to America. Guide students through the written activities. Discuss their responses.

Ask:

1. *What happened after Christopher Columbus arrived in America?* (Other immigrants began to come to America.) **L1**

2. *Why did immigrants come to America?* (Some came looking for land, gold, adventure, and to find freedom.) **L2**

3. *Why do you think life changed for both Native Americans and immigrants as the settlements grew?* **L3**

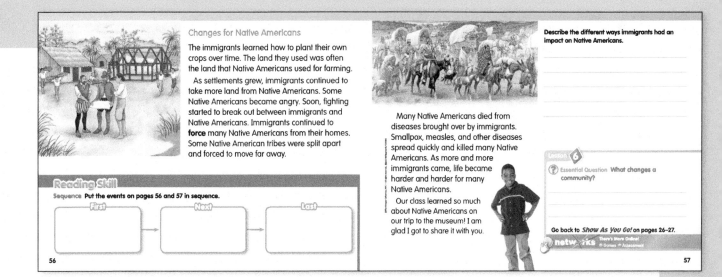

Changes for Native Americans

The immigrants learned how to plant their own crops over time. The land they used was often the land that Native Americans used for farming.

As settlements grew, immigrants continued to take more land from Native Americans. Some Native Americans became angry. Soon, fighting started to break out between immigrants and Native Americans. Immigrants continued to **force** many Native Americans from their homes. Some Native American tribes were split apart and forced to move far away.

Reading Skill

Sequence Put the events on pages 56 and 57 in sequence.

First → Next → Last

56

Describe the different ways immigrants had an impact on Native Americans.

_____
_____
_____
_____

Many Native Americans died from diseases brought over by immigrants. Smallpox, measles, and other diseases spread quickly and killed many Native Americans. As more and more immigrants came, life became harder and harder for many Native Americans.

Our class learned so much about Native Americans on our trip to the museum! I am glad I got to share it with you.

Lesson 6

? Essential Question What changes a community?

_____
_____

Go back to *Show As You Go!* on pages 26–27.

network

57

Active Teaching

Read the pages together. Have small groups discuss how life changed for Native Americans and immigrants. Guide students as they complete the written activities, except for the Essential Question. Discuss their responses.

Develop Comprehension

Ask:

1. *How did life change for Native Americans?* (They were forced from their homes. Many Native Americans died from diseases brought over by the immigrants.) **L2**

2. *How did life change for immigrants?* (They had to learn how to survive in a new land.) **L2**

3. *Why were Native Americans forced from their homelands?* (The immigrants took over their land for their homes and farms.) **L2**

Use the leveled reader to extend and enrich students' understanding of the impact of immigrants on the Native Americans. A lesson plan for this leveled reader can be found on pages T18–T19 at the front of this Teacher Edition.

Then revisit the KWL chart from the beginning of the unit. Have students fill in the last column of the chart with what they learned about Native Americans. Then have students respond to the Essential Question. Discuss their responses. Have students revisit their response on page 54 and compare it to their response at the end of the lesson. Discuss how their answers changed.

Show As You Go! Remind students to go back to complete the project on the Unit Opener.

Reading Skill

Common Core Standard RI.3: Describe the connection between a series of historical events, scientific ideas or concepts, or steps in technical procedures in a text.

Sequence Discuss students' responses to the sequencing activity on page 56. Explain to students that the words *first*, *next*, and *last* signal a sequence of events. Have students practice using the words *first*, *next*, and *last* as they describe their morning routines.

Response to Intervention

? Essential Question **What changes a community?**

If . . . students cannot give a substantiated response to the Essential Question, "What changes a community?"

. . . .

Then . . . have students discuss why life changed for Native Americans and immigrants. Following the discussion, allow students to respond to the Essential Question again.

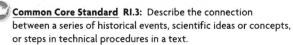

Go to connected.mcgraw-hill.com for additional resources:

- Interactive Whiteboard Lessons
- Worksheets
- Assessment

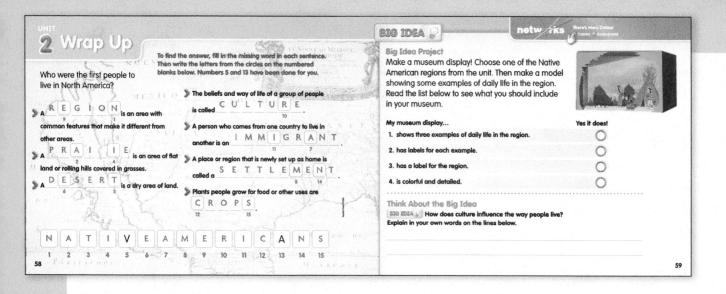

Wrap Up

Word Puzzle Have students complete page 58 with a partner to review the unit vocabulary.

BIG IDEA Big Idea Project

Students will be making a mini museum display to show what they learned in Unit 2.

- Read the checklist together and answer students' questions about the project.
- Have students revisit the *Show As You Go!* pages for information from each lesson.
- Provide supplies such as boxes, cardboard, construction paper, markers, and tape.
- Have students share their mini museum display with the class.
- Then display the mini museums in the classroom to remind students of what they learned about Native American cultures.
- After students complete their projects, encourage self-reflection by asking:
  - How did you plan your mini museum display?
  - What changes would you make to this project if you did it again? What did you learn from making your mini museum display?
- To assess the project, refer to the rubric on the following page.

Differentiated Instruction

▶ **Approaching** Allow students to print images from the Internet to use in their displays. Have them describe the elements in their display as you write their words.

▶ **Beyond** Have pairs do oral presentations about how the cultures they represented in their display are the same and different.

▶ **ELL** Have students describe the elements in their display to a partner. Have them work with their partner to write sentences about each element.

Response to Intervention

BIG IDEA Culture influences the way people live.

If . . . students cannot give a substantiated response to the Big Idea, "Culture influences the way people live"

. . . .

Then . . . discuss with students what was the same and different about each Native American culture. Discuss how the environment affected the daily life of each culture. Following the discussion, allow students to respond to the Big Idea again.

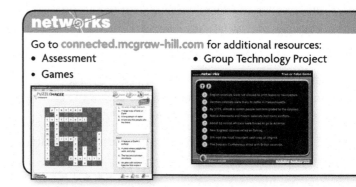

networks

Go to **connected.mcgraw-hill.com** for additional resources:
- Assessment
- Games
- Group Technology Project

Name _____ Date _____

Mini Museum Display Rubric

4 Exemplary	3 Accomplished	2 Developing	1 Beginning
The museum:	**The museum:**	**The museum:**	**The museum:**
☐ includes all required checklist items as well as additional information	☐ includes all required checklist items	☐ includes all but 1 of the required checklist items	☐ is missing several required checklist items
☐ has all items clearly labeled	☐ has almost all items clearly labeled	☐ has some items clearly labeled	☐ has few items labeled
☐ includes accurate facts about the Native American culture that is represented	☐ includes at least 2 accurate facts about the Native American culture that is represented	☐ includes at least 1 accurate fact about the Native American culture that is represented	☐ has no accurate facts about the Native American culture that is represented
☐ contains few, if any, errors in capitalization and spelling	☐ contains some errors in capitalization and spelling	☐ contains several errors in capitalization and spelling	☐ contains serious errors in capitalization and spelling

Grading Comments: _____

_____

_____

_____

_____

_____

_____

_____

_____

_____

Project Score: _____

UNIT 3 Planner A LAND OF IMMIGRANTS

BIG IDEA 💡 **Change happens over time.**

Student Portfolio

- **Show As You Go!**
  Use these pages to introduce the Big Idea. Students record information specific to each lesson. They use these pages to help them plan their Big Idea Project.

net**w**rks

- **Group Technology Project**
  Students use 21ˢᵗ century skills to complete a group extension activity of the unit project. Lesson plans, worksheets and rubrics are available online.

Student Portfolio

- **Big Idea Project**
  Students will work together to plan and create a poster to show things that make up their culture. The Big Idea Project rubric is on page 87W.

Reading Skills

Student Portfolio

- **Reading Skill: Understanding Sequence**
  Pages 62–63. Common Core State Standards RI.3

net**w**rks

- **Skill Builders**
  Introduce and practice the reading skill.

Leveled Readers

Use the leveled reader, (lesson plan on pages T20–T21) with Lesson 2 and *The Supreme Court* (lesson plan on pages T22–T23) with Lesson 3.

Treasures Connection

Teach this unit with Treasures Unit 1, *My Name is Yoon*, pages 116–142.

Social Studies Skills

Student Portfolio

- **Primary Sources: Photographs**
  Page 67

net**w**rks

- **Skill Builders**
  Introduce and teach analyzing primary and secondary sources.

Activity Cards

- **Center for Social Studies Skills Investigation**
  Use the center activity cards to help students explore Primary Sources, Geography, and Citizenship.

FOLDABLES®

Student Portfolio

- Students can create vocabulary Foldables right in their portfolios.

Assessment Solutions

- **McGraw-Hill networks™**
  Safe online testing features multiple question types that are easy to use and editable!

- **Self-Check Quizzes**

- **Worksheets**

UNIT 3 **At a Glance**

	Lesson	Essential Question	Vocabulary	Digital Resources
1	**Colonial America**	**How do communities change over time?**	colony colonist *ruled	Go to **connected.mcgraw-hill.com** for additional resources: • Interactive Whiteboard Lessons • Worksheets • Assessment • Lesson Plans • Content Library • Skill Builders • Videos • Use Standards Tracker on **networks** to track students' progress
2	**Coming to America**	**Why do people move?**	Statue of Liberty Ellis Island *escape	
3	**Sharing Culture**	**How does culture shape a community?**	contribution custom *blend	

*denotes academic vocabulary

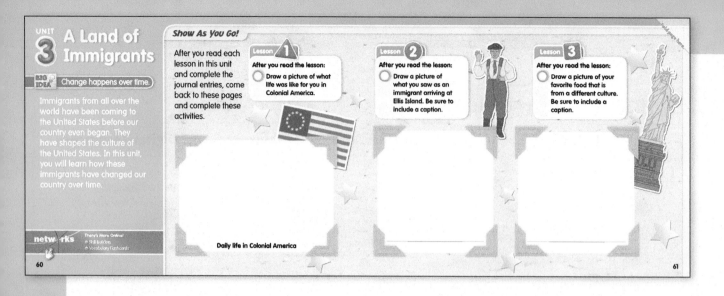

UNIT
3 A Land of Immigrants

BIG IDEA Change happens over time.

Immigrants from all over the world have been coming to the United States before our country even began. They have shaped the culture of the United States. In this unit, you will learn how these immigrants have changed our country over time.

networks
There's More Online!
• Skill Builders
• Vocabulary Flashcards

60

Show As You Go!

After you read each lesson in this unit and complete the journal entries, come back to these pages and complete these activities.

Lesson 1

After you read the lesson:
○ Draw a picture of what life was like for you in Colonial America.

Lesson 2

After you read the lesson:
○ Draw a picture of what you saw as an immigrant arriving at Ellis Island. Be sure to include a caption.

Lesson 3

After you read the lesson:
○ Draw a picture of your favorite food that is from a different culture. Be sure to include a caption.

Daily life in Colonial America

61

Introduce the Unit

☑ Diagnostic Assessment

Ask: What do you know about immigrants who have come to the United States?

Read aloud the statements below.

Students respond to indicate familiarity with each statement by holding up fingers with:

1 = I know very little about this.

2 = I know a lot about this.

- I know about Colonial America.
- I know about the Statue of Liberty.
- I know about Ellis Island.
- I know about the contributions immigrants have made to our country.

Students' responses will help identify their level of understanding.

Active Teaching

BIG IDEA **Change happens over time.**

In this unit, students will learn about the immigrants who have brought change to the United States over time. Students will use the *Show As You Go!* pages throughout their study of this unit. Students will use information from each lesson to complete the activities.

At this point, have students fold back the corner of page 61. This will help them flip back to this page as needed. Explain to students that at the end of the unit, they will use the information collected on these pages to complete the Big Idea Project.

Differentiated Instruction

▶ **Approaching** Review the directions under each lesson head to help students identify what they should be looking for as they read. Have them underline the things they need to draw in the boxes. As lessons are completed, allow them to work in small groups to draw their pictures.

▶ **Beyond** Have students write a label and brief description for each of their pictures.

▶ **ELL** Have students circle key words in the directions. Define unfamiliar words. As lessons are completed, have students work with a partner to discuss and record information on the pages.

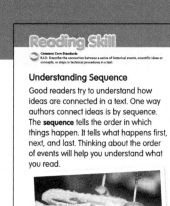

Common Core Standards
RI.3: Describe the connection between a series of historical events, scientific ideas or concepts, or steps in technical procedures in a text.

Understanding Sequence

Good readers try to understand how ideas are connected in a text. One way authors connect ideas is by sequence. The **sequence** tells the order in which things happen. It tells what happens first, next, and last. Thinking about the order of events will help you understand what you read.

Learn It

To understand sequence:

1. Look for clue words such as first, next, later, and last. These words can help show the order of events.

2. Look for dates that tell exactly when things happened.

Paula made a Cuban Sandwich for her friend. First she toasted two slices of bread. Next she spread mustard on one slice of bread and layered it with slices of pork and ham. Then she added melted Swiss cheese and pickles. Last she topped it with a buttered piece of bread and gave it to her friend.

What happened first

What happened next

What happened last

Try It

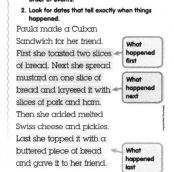

You can use the chart below to write events in sequence. Write the events in order from the story on page 62.

First
Paula toasted the bread.

↓

Next
She spread mustard on one slice of bread and layered it with slices of pork and ham.

↓

Last
She topped the layers with buttered bread and gave it to her friend.

Apply It

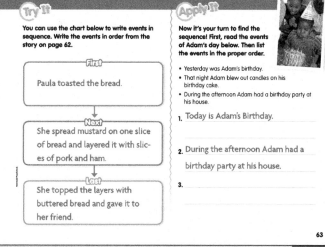

Now it's your turn to find the sequence! First, read the events of Adam's day below. Then list the events in the proper order.

• Yesterday was Adam's birthday.
• That night Adam blew out candles on his birthday cake.
• During the afternoon Adam had a birthday party at his house.

1. Today is Adam's Birthday.

2. During the afternoon Adam had a birthday party at his house.

3. _____

62   63

 Common Core Standards RI.3: Describe the connection between a series of historical events, scientific ideas or concepts, or steps in technical procedures in a text.

Reading Skill

Active Teaching

LEARN IT Understanding Sequence

Read **LEARN IT** together. Discuss the definition of sequence.

Say: *As I read, I think, "What is the order of events?" This strategy helps me to identify the sequence of the story. Being able to identify sequence helps me to understand how events in a story are connected.*

TRY IT Encourage students to try the modeled strategy as they complete the **TRY IT** activity.

APPLY IT After students have completed the **APPLY IT** activity,

Ask:

1. *What question should you ask yourself to help find the sequence?* (What is the order of events?) **L1**

2. *What can help you find the sequence in a story?* (clue words such as *first*, *next*, and *last*, as well as dates) **L2**

3. *Why is it important to identify the sequence of a story?* **L3**

Differentiated Instruction

▶ **Approaching** Review the **LEARN IT** activity as a small group. Do the **TRY IT** activity together. Have students complete the **APPLY IT** activity independently. Regroup to compare and correct.

▶ **Beyond** Provide a variety of short stories for students to find the sequence of events. Have them complete a sequence graphic organizer for the stories they examine. Have students explain their work to a partner.

▶ **ELL** Have students dramatize the stories on pages 62 and 63. Engage students in a discussion about what happened in each story. Explain that *first*, *next*, and *last* are clue words that can help show the order of events. Have students state the order of events in each story.

networks

Go to connected.mcgraw-hill.com for additional resources:
• Skill Builders
• Graphic Organizers

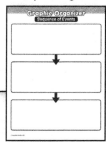

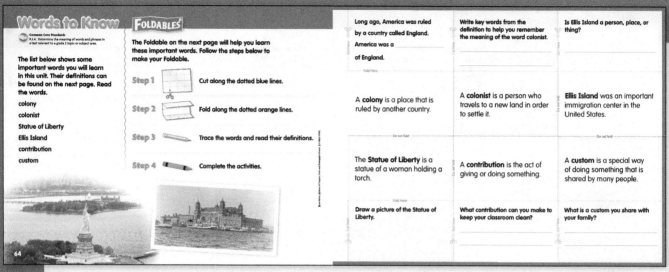

Common Core Standards
RI.4: Determine the meaning of words and phrases in a text relevant to a grade 2 topic or subject area.

The list below shows some important words you will learn in this unit. Their definitions can be found on the next page. Read the words.

colony
colonist
Statue of Liberty
Ellis Island
contribution
custom

The Foldable on the next page will help you learn these important words. Follow the steps below to make your Foldable.

Step 1 — Cut along the dotted blue lines.

Step 2 — Fold along the dotted orange lines.

Step 3 — Trace the words and read their definitions.

Step 4 — Complete the activities.

Long ago, America was ruled by a country called England. America was a _____ of England.

Write key words from the definition to help you remember the meaning of the word colonist.

Is Ellis Island a person, place, or thing?

A **colony** is a place that is ruled by another country.

A **colonist** is a person who travels to a new land in order to settle it.

Ellis Island was an important immigration center in the United States.

The **Statue of Liberty** is a statue of a woman holding a torch.

A **contribution** is the act of giving or doing something.

A **custom** is a special way of doing something that is shared by many people.

Draw a picture of the Statue of Liberty.

What contribution can you make to keep your classroom clean?

What is a custom you share with your family?

64

Common Core Standards **RI.4:** Determine the meaning of words and phrases in a text relevant to a grade 2 topic or subject area.

Words to Know

Active Teaching

1. Go to connected.mcgraw-hill.com for flashcards to introduce the unit vocabulary to students.

2. Read the words on the list on page 64 and have students repeat them after you.

3. Guide students as they complete steps 1 through 4 of the Foldable.

4. Have students use the Foldable to practice the vocabulary words independently or with a partner.

networks

Go to connected.mcgraw-hill.com for additional resources:
- Vocabulary Flashcards
- Vocabulary Games
- Graphic Organizers

GO Vocabulary!
Use the graphic organizer below to help students practice the meaning of the words from the list. Have students pick a word. Then ask them to write down three other terms or words they know that can be associated with their particular word. Students should explain why they listed the words that they did. Next, have them discuss with a partner other words that may have been listed. Continue the exercise with all of the words on the list.

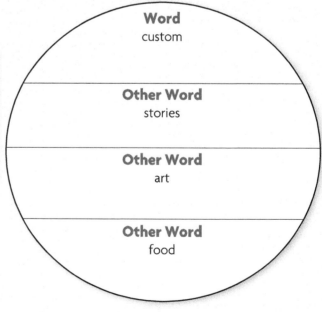

Word
custom

Other Word
stories

Other Word
art

Other Word
food

Primary Sources

Photographs are one type of primary source. A photograph is a picture that is taken with a camera. People have been using cameras and taking pictures for many years. Photographs from long ago can show us what life was like way back then. We can learn about how people lived and the places they went long ago.

Document-Based Questions

1. What do you see going on in this photograph?

2. How can you tell this photograph is from long ago?

This is a photograph of immigrants arriving at Ellis Island in 1904.

networks
There's More Online!
• Skill Builders
• Resource Library

67

Differentiated Instruction

▶ **ELL** Write the vocabulary words from the Foldable on the board. Discuss the relationship among these terms with students.

W O R D P L A Y

Play Word Whacker to help students practice the vocabulary.

- Create a word wall by listing all of the words from the list on the board.
- Have students select a word from the list and write a definition in their own words on a 3 x 5 card.
- Ask students to sign their names to the cards and pass them in.
- Two students stand at the word wall with a fly swatter or a rolled up newspaper to compete with each other.
- Read the definitions aloud.
- As the definitions are read, the students try to 'whack' the correct word first.
- If there are issues with the definitions as stated on the card, the class can offer corrections so that the student who wrote the definition can improve his or her understanding of the word.
- Repeat the steps above with the rest of the words. Allow students to take turns whacking the words.

Primary Sources

Active Teaching

Explain to students that the image on the page shows immigrants going through Ellis Island in 1904. Use page 67 to teach your students about using photographs to learn about people, places, and events in the past. Read the page together. Discuss the difference between black and white photographs and color photographs. Talk about how black and white photographs can look dated. Then guide students through the written activities.

Ask: *What can we learn about life in the past from photographs?* **L3**

networks

Go to **connected.mcgraw-hill.com** for additional resources:

- Skill Builders
- Resource Library

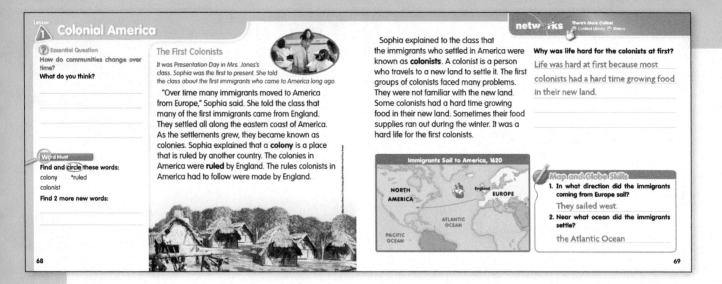

Activate Prior Knowledge

Say: *Colonial children did not have much free time, but when they did, they came up with a lot of ways to have fun. They played games such as tag, leapfrog, and hide-and-seek.*

Play a game called "Deer and Hunter" to teach students about daily life during colonial times.

- The players, or hunters, stand in a circle holding hands.
- The 'deer' weaves in and out of the circle, under the hands of the players.
- When the deer taps one of the hunters, the hunter must follow the deer and imitate its movements.
- If the hunter catches the deer before it has gone around the circle once, the deer goes into the middle of the circle.
- If the hunter doesn't catch the deer or doesn't imitate its movements exactly, the hunter goes into the middle of the circle.
- The game continues until the players on the outside of the circle can't encircle the players inside the circle.

Tell students that in this lesson they will be learn more about daily life in Colonial America.

? Essential Question How do communities change over time?

Have students explain what they understand about the Essential Question. Discuss their responses. Explain that everything they learn in this lesson will help them understand the Essential Question better. Remind them to think about how the Essential Question connects to the unit Big Idea: Change happens over time.

Active Teaching

Words To Know Have students look through the lesson to find the words that are listed in the Word Hunt. Then have them read the definitions of the content vocabulary words and use context clues or the glossary to determine the meaning of the academic vocabulary word. To increase students' understanding of the word, ask them what they think it would be like if the United States was ruled by another country today.

Develop Comprehension

Read and discuss the pages together to help students learn about life for the first immigrants in America. Guide students through the written activities. Discuss their responses.

Ask:

1. *What is a colony?* (a place that is ruled by another country) **L1**

2. *What problems did the first groups of colonists face?* (They did not know how to hunt and grow food and sometimes their food supplies ran out.) **L2**

3. *What do you think your life would be like if you were a colonist?* **L3**

Map and Globe Skill

For additional practice, have students identify where the immigrants sailing to America came from on a classroom map.

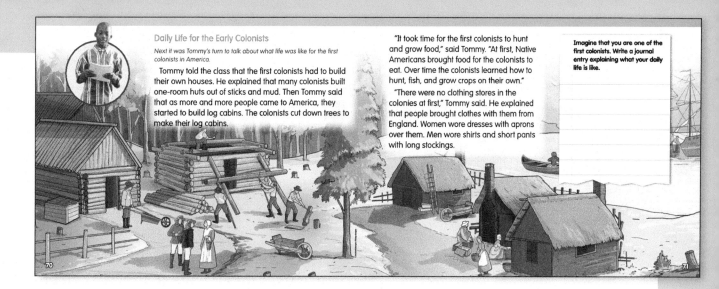

Daily Life for the Early Colonists

Next it was Tommy's turn to talk about what life was like for the first colonists in America.

Tommy told the class that the first colonists had to build their own houses. He explained that many colonists built one-room huts out of sticks and mud. Then Tommy said that as more and more people came to America, they started to build log cabins. The colonists cut down trees to make their log cabins.

"It took time for the first colonists to hunt and grow food," said Tommy. "At first, Native Americans brought food for the colonists to eat. Over time the colonists learned how to hunt, fish, and grow crops on their own."

"There were no clothing stores in the colonies at first," Tommy said. He explained that people brought clothes with them from England. Women wore dresses with aprons over them. Men wore shirts and short pants with long stockings.

Imagine that you are one of the first colonists. Write a journal entry explaining what your daily life is like.

Active Teaching

Read the pages together to help students learn about daily life for the early colonists. Guide students through the written activities. Discuss their journal responses.

Develop Comprehension

Ask:

1. *How did Native Americans help the colonists at first?* (They brought them food.) **L1**

2. *How did colonists use the land around them for housing and food?* **L3**

DID YOU KNOW?

Ask: *Did you know that children in Colonial America helped their parents with many of the daily chores?*

Tell students that children helped adults with much of the farm work. Milking cows and gathering things to fuel the cook stove were a duty for both girls and boys. Girls helped with the cooking, cleaning, mending, gathering eggs, and taking care of the younger children. Boys helped with the planting and harvesting and with hunting for food to feed the family.

☑ Formative Assessment

Have students summarize what they know about daily life in early Colonial America. Have them draw a picture or write a brief description. Use this assessment to monitor students' understanding and identify the need for intervention.

Differentiated Instruction

▶ **Approaching** Have students draw a picture showing something they learned about daily life in early Colonial America.

▶ **Beyond** Have students write a short paragraph comparing their daily life to that of an early colonist's daily life.

▶ **ELL** Have students look at the picture on these pages. Point to each item in the picture and ask students to tell you what it is.

netw⊙rks

Go to connected.mcgraw-hill.com for additional resources:

- Interactive Whiteboard Lessons
- Assessment
- Lesson Plans
- Worksheets

My State on the Map

Look at the map. Color your state green. Do any other states touch your state? Color them orange.

How many states touch your state?

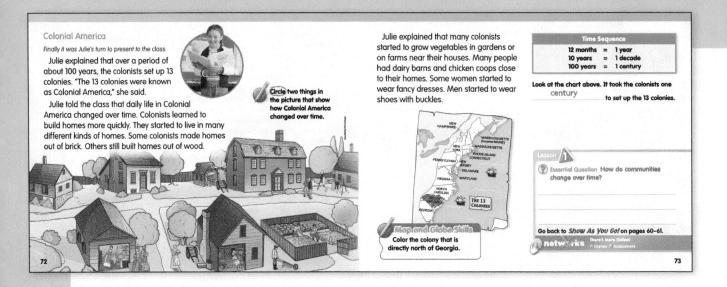

Colonial America

Finally it was Julie's turn to present to the class.

Julie explained that over a period of about 100 years, the colonists set up 13 colonies. "The 13 colonies were known as Colonial America," she said.

Julie told the class that daily life in Colonial America changed over time. Colonists learned to build homes more quickly. They started to live in many different kinds of homes. Some colonists made homes out of brick. Others still built homes out of wood.

Circle two things in the picture that show how Colonial America changed over time.

Julie explained that many colonists started to grow vegetables in gardens or on farms near their houses. Many people had dairy barns and chicken coops close to their homes. Some women started to wear fancy dresses. Men started to wear shoes with buckles.

Time Sequence		
12 months	=	1 year
10 years	=	1 decade
100 years	=	1 century

Look at the chart above. It took the colonists one ___century___ to set up the 13 colonies.

Map and Globe Skills
Color the colony that is directly north of Georgia.

Lesson 1
? Essential Question How do communities change over time?

Go back to *Show As You Go!* on pages 60–61.

networks *There's More Online!*
Games • Assessment

Lesson 1

Active Teaching

Before students read, ask them to think about how life changed for the colonists. Read the pages together. Guide students through the written activities. Discuss their responses.

Develop Comprehension

Ask:

1. *How many colonies were set up over a period of 100 years?* (13) **L1**

2. *How did the colonists improve their homes over time?* (They learned to work together to build their homes more quickly and they built them stronger.) **L2**

3. *How did daily life change over time in Colonial America?* **L3**

Summarize the lesson with the class. Then have students respond to the Essential Question. Discuss their responses. Have students revisit their response on page 68 and compare it to their response at the end of the lesson. Discuss how their answers changed.

> **Show As You Go!** Remind students to go back to the Unit Opener and complete the activities for this lesson.

Map and Globe Skill

For additional practice, have students identify other colonies on the map and color them in.

Response to Intervention

? **Essential Question How do communities change over time?**

If . . . students cannot give a substantiated response to the Essential Question, "How do communities change over time?"

. . . .

Then . . . take students back to pages 68 through 73. Have them look at the pictures. Then discuss the many things that changed over time in Colonial America.

Ask: *How did housing, food, and clothing change over time in Colonial America?.*

Following the discussion, allow students to respond to the Essential Question again.

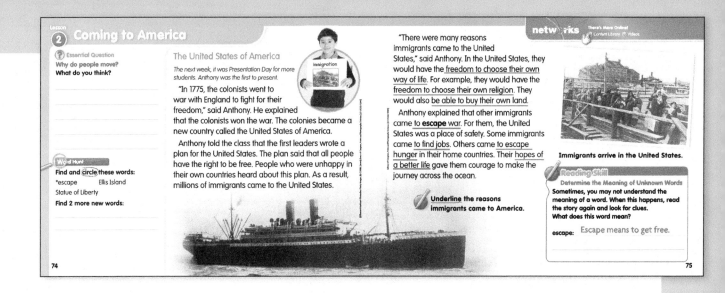

Essential Question
Why do people move?
What do you think?

Word Hunt
Find and circle these words:
*escape   Ellis Island
Statue of Liberty
Find 2 more new words:

The United States of America

The next week, it was Presentation Day for more students. Anthony was the first to present.

"In 1775, the colonists went to war with England to fight for their freedom," said Anthony. He explained that the colonists won the war. The colonies became a new country called the United States of America.

Anthony told the class that the first leaders wrote a plan for the United States. The plan said that all people have the right to be free. People who were unhappy in their own countries heard about this plan. As a result, millions of immigrants came to the United States.

"There were many reasons immigrants came to the United States," said Anthony. In the United States, they would have the freedom to choose their own way of life. For example, they would have the freedom to choose their own religion. They would also be able to buy their own land.

Anthony explained that other immigrants came to **escape** war. For them, the United States was a place of safety. Some immigrants came to find jobs. Others came to escape hunger in their home countries. Their hopes of a better life gave them courage to make the journey across the ocean.

Underline the reasons immigrants came to America.

Immigrants arrive in the United States.

Reading Skill
Determine the Meaning of Unknown Words
Sometimes, you may not understand the meaning of a word. When this happens, read the story again and look for clues.
What does this word mean?
escape: Escape means to get free.

74   75

Lesson 2

Activate Prior Knowledge

Give each student a large brown bag. Tell them they are going to another country.

Instruct them that they cannot bring anything with them that will not fit into their bag. Have them go home and decide what possessions they would like to take with them. Have students list their possessions on the front of the bag.

Tape off sections of floor in the classroom, measuring about 3 x 5 ft, for each student. Tell students their square is where they are to place their belongings. They may not put any of their stuff outside of their square. It may get confusing and noisy, but that is okay.

Explain to students that immigrants who traveled to the United States in the late 1800s and early 1900s had very little room on the ships taking them to the United States. Tell them that the immigrants only had about the same amount of room as where they are standing now.

Say: *In this lesson, you will learn more about these immigrants.*

? Essential Question   Why do people move?

Have students explain what they understand about the Essential Question. Discuss their responses. Explain that everything they learn in this lesson will help them understand the Essential Question better. Remind them to think about how the Essential Question connects to the unit Big Idea: Change happens over time.

Active Teaching

Words To Know Have students look through the lesson to find the words that are listed in the Word Hunt. Then have them read the definitions of the content vocabulary words and use context clues or the glossary to determine the meaning of the academic vocabulary word. To increase students' understanding of the word, ask them to use the word in other sentences.

Develop Comprehension

Read and discuss the pages together to help students learn about the reasons immigrants came to America. Guide students through the written activities. Discuss their journal responses.

Ask:

1. *What happened after the colonists won the war?* (The colonies became a new country called the United States of America.) **L1**

2. *What did the plan for the United States say?* (that all people should be treated fairly) **L2**

3. *Why do you think freedom is important?* **L3**

Reading Skill

Common Core Standards RI.4: Determine the meaning of words and phrases in a text relevant to a grade 2 topic or subject area.

Determine Meaning of Unknown Words For additional practice, ask students to list other words they may not know the meaning of. Have them use context clues or a dictionary to help them determine the meaning of the words.

Arriving in the United States

Next it was Lena's turn to present her report.

Lena said that between the years 1892 and 1954, millions of immigrants came to the United States. Many came in ships through New York Harbor. As the immigrants entered the harbor, they could see the **Statue of Liberty**.

"The Statue of Liberty is a large statue that was a gift from France. It is located on Liberty Island in New York Harbor," said Lena. "The Statue of Liberty stands for the freedoms we have in the United States."

///////// GLUE FOLDABLE HERE /////////

Statue of Liberty · Ellis Island

New York

76

"The first place many immigrants went before they began their lives in America was **Ellis Island**," said Lena. "Ellis Island was an important immigration center in New York Harbor. The center was opened on January 1, 1892, so that immigration officials could find out how many people were arriving in America."

The Statue of Liberty was shipped from France in pieces and put together in the United States. It took over four months to finish!

Imagine you are an immigrant arriving in New York Harbor. Write a journal entry telling what you see and feel. Explain why the Statue of Liberty is important to you.

77

Lesson 2

Active Teaching

Read the pages together to help students learn about the Statue of Liberty and Ellis Island. Guide students through the written activities. Discuss their journal responses.

Develop Comprehension

Ask:

1. *What does the Statue of Liberty stand for?* (the freedoms we have in the United States) **L1**

2. *Why do you think the Statue of Liberty was a welcome sight to many immigrants?* **L3**

3. *Why was an immigration center needed in the United States?* **L3**

More About the Statue of Liberty A French artist named Frederic-Auguste Bartholdi drew up the plans for the Statue of Liberty in 1874. Workers in France used copper sheets for the statue's outside surface, or skin. When the Statue of Liberty was first built, she was reddish brown—the color of new copper. Copper changes color when it is first left outside. It turns a light green or blue. That is why she is the color she is today. The Statue of Liberty is 305 feet tall, as tall as a 30-story building. The burning torch stands for truth and serves as a welcome to voyagers. The crown has 7 points. Each point stands for the 7 seas and the 7 continents of the world. She is holding a tablet with the date July 4, 1776, written on it, the day the Declaration of Independence was approved.

☑ Formative Assessment

Ask students true and false questions about immigration and the Statue of Liberty. Use this assessment to monitor students' understanding and identify need for intervention.

Ask:

- Immigrants are people who leave one country to live in another. (T)
- Many immigrants came to America looking for a better life. (T)
- All immigrants speak English. (F)
- Ellis Island is a popular vacation spot for immigrants. (F)
- The Statue of Liberty is a symbol of freedom to many immigrants. (T)

Page Power

FOLDABLES Interact more with the page. Have students create a Foldable to assist them in developing their understanding of the Statue of Liberty.

1. Provide students with a copy of Foldable 3A from the Notebook Foldables section at the back of this book.

2. Have students construct the Foldable and glue its anchor tab above the Statue of Liberty on page 76.

3. On the Foldable flaps have students write 2 facts about the Statue of Liberty that they learned from the text.

4. On the backs of the flaps, have students list 2 more facts about the Statue of Liberty that they find from other texts in the school library or on the Internet.

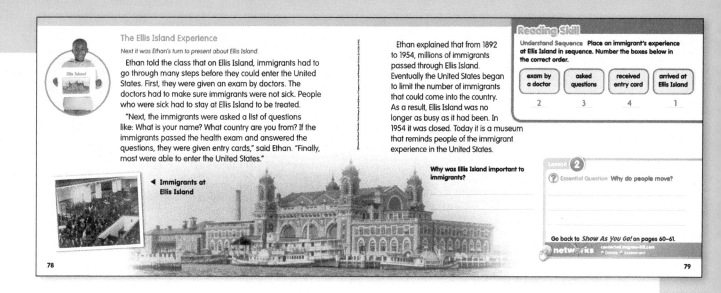

The Ellis Island Experience

Next it was Ethan's turn to present about Ellis Island.

Ethan told the class that on Ellis Island, immigrants had to go through many steps before they could enter the United States. First, they were given an exam by doctors. The doctors had to make sure immigrants were not sick. People who were sick had to stay at Ellis Island to be treated.

"Next, the immigrants were asked a list of questions like: What is your name? What country are you from? If the immigrants passed the health exam and answered the questions, they were given entry cards," said Ethan. "Finally, most were able to enter the United States."

◀ **Immigrants at Ellis Island**

Ethan explained that from 1892 to 1954, millions of immigrants passed through Ellis Island. Eventually the United States began to limit the number of immigrants that could come into the country. As a result, Ellis Island was no longer as busy as it had been. In 1954 it was closed. Today it is a museum that reminds people of the immigrant experience in the United States.

Why was Ellis Island important to immigrants?

Understand Sequence Place an immigrant's experience at Ellis Island in sequence. Number the boxes below in the correct order.

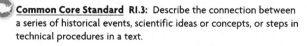

exam by a doctor	asked questions	received entry card	arrived at Ellis Island
2	3	4	1

Lesson 2

(?) **Essential Question** Why do people move?

Go back to *Show As You Go!* on pages 60–61.

78   79

Active Teaching

Read the pages together to help students understand the importance of Ellis Island. Guide students through the written activities. Discuss their journal responses.

Develop Comprehension

Ask:

1. *What did immigrants have to do when they first arrived at Ellis Island?* (have a health exam by a doctor) **L1**

2. *Why did immigrants need to have a health exam?* (Doctors had to make sure that immigrants were not bringing diseases into the United States.) **L2**

3. *How do you think immigrants felt after they were given their entry cards?* **L3**

Summarize the lesson with the class. Then have students respond to the Essential Question. Discuss students' responses. Have students revisit their response on page 74 and compare it to their response at the end of the lesson. Discuss how their answers changed.

Use the leveled reader, *Annie Moore: Ellis Island's First Immigrant*, to extend and enrich students' understanding of an immigrant's experience at Ellis Island. A lesson plan for this leveled reader can be found on pages T20–T21 at the front of this Teacher Edition.

Show As You Go! Remind students to go back to the Unit Opener and complete the activities for this lesson.

Reading Skill

Common Core Standard RI.3: Describe the connection between a series of historical events, scientific ideas or concepts, or steps in technical procedures in a text.

Understand Sequence For additional practice, ask students to list the sequence of events in their school day.

Response to Intervention

(?) **Essential Question** **Why do people move?**

If . . . students cannot give a substantiated response to the Essential Question, "Why do people move?"

Then . . . take students back to pages 74 through 79. Discuss the reasons why people came to the United States.

Ask: *What are some reasons immigrants came to the United States?*

Following the discussion, allow students to respond to the Essential Question again.

networks

Go to connected.mcgraw-hill.com for additional resources:

- Interactive Whiteboard Lessons
- Worksheets
- Assessment
- Videos

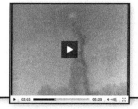

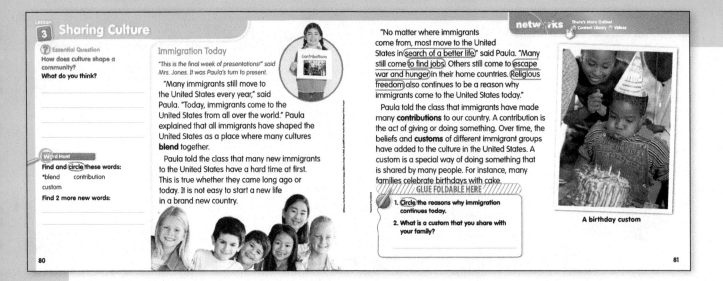

Lesson 3

Activate Prior Knowledge

Share your ethnic background with the class. Then have students share their ethnic backgrounds with the class. Have a discussion comparing the different backgrounds of the people in your class. Tell students that in this lesson they will learn more about how immigrants have shaped the United States as a place where many cultures blend together.

(?) Essential Question How does culture shape a community?

Have students explain what they understand about the Essential Question. Discuss their responses. Explain that everything they learn in this lesson will help them understand the Essential Question better. Remind them to think about how the Essential Question connects to the unit Big Idea: Change happens over time.

Page Power

FOLDABLES® Interact more with the page. Have students create a Foldable to assist them in developing their understanding of customs.

1. Provide students with a copy of Foldable 3A from the Notebook Foldables section at the back of this book.

2. Have students construct the Foldable and glue its anchor tab over the question on page 81.

3. On the Foldable flap, have students draw a picture of the custom they share with their family.

4. Under the flap, have students explain why it is a custom.

Active Teaching

 Have students look through the lesson to find the words that are listed in the Word Hunt. Then have them read the definitions of the content vocabulary words and use context clues or the glossary to determine the meanings of the academic vocabulary word. To increase students' understanding of the word, ask them to think about examples of things that can blend together.

Develop Comprehension

Read and discuss the page together to help students learn about the reasons immigrants still come to the United States today. Guide students through the written activities. Discuss their journal responses.

Ask:

1. *What is culture?* (the beliefs and way of life of a group of people) **L1**

2. *What are some reasons immigrants continue to come to the United States today?* **L2**

3. *What are some contributions immigrants have made to our country?* **L3**

Urban Communities

There are three kinds of communities. A city, like New York, is an **urban** community. Urban communities have many tall buildings and stores. The streets and sidewalks are busy with people, cars, buses, and taxis.

What are some features of a city?

Suburban Communities

A community near a city is called a suburban community. **Suburban** communities are less crowded than urban areas. There are not as many places to work. People might even travel to the urban community to work.

Rural Communities

Rural communities are far from cities. These areas have lots of open land. It might take a long time to get to school or the store. There are a lot of farms in rural communities.

What type of community would you most like to live in? Why?

Active Teaching

Read pages 82-83 together. Have small groups discuss how life would be different depending upon where people live. Guide students as they answer the questions.

Have them repeat the vocabulary words after you. Then have students list the things that they would find in each area.

Develop Comprehension

Ask:

1. *What is the difference between a city and a suburb?* **L1**

2. *How is a city different from a rural area?* **L1**

3. *How is a suburb different from a rural area?* **L1**

4. *Would you prefer to live in a suburban or rural area? Why?*

Differentiated Instruction

▶ **Approaching** Have students review the lesson and create one question for each page.

▶ **Beyond** Have students write a brief story about living in one type of community.

▶ **ELL** Show the students pictures of each type of community. Then draw a circle with four quadrants. Write the title Urban, Suburban, or Rural above the circle. Have students think of words to describe the area in each community type and write them in the four quadrants of the concept circle.

Paula continued with her presentation. She had researched how other cultures have added to the culture of the United States.

Paula took pictures of things she saw in her neighborhood. She made a poster to show how other cultures have influenced things like food, music, clothing, art, language, and celebrations.

Think about other foods, music, and clothing from different cultures. Describe one of them in a journal entry.

This picture shows an Italian restaurant in our neighborhood. Long ago, Americans did not eat spaghetti. Immigrants from Italy made it popular in our country. Today Americans enjoy making spaghetti at home and eating it in restaurants.

My family and I took a walk in our neighborhood, and we noticed a group of people playing jazz music. Africans who came to the United States brought songs and rhythms with them. Musicians in the United States changed the music and turned it into jazz. Jazz, blues, and hip hop are just some of the kinds of music we listen to today that grew out of African music.

Mrs. Ross, our librarian, was wearing a shirt made out of silk. Silk cloth was invented in China. Many Chinese immigrants brought silk with them when they came to the United States. Silk is very soft and is used today to make clothing.

84

85

Active Teaching

Before students read, have them think about how other cultures have influenced the culture of the United States. Read the pages together. Guide students through the written activities. Discuss their journal responses.

Develop Comprehension

Ask:

1. *What cultures are shown on pages 82 and 83?* (Italian, African, Chinese) **L1**

2. *What types of music grew out of African music?* (jazz, blues, hip hop) **L1**

3. *What is something from a different culture that you have noticed in your everyday life?* **L3**

Page Power

Interact more with the page. Have students:

• write down other examples from different cultures for each image on the page.

• draw one of their other examples next to the image.

Differentiated Instruction

▶ **ELL** Have students circle the contributions from each country shown on pages 82 to 85.

☑ Formative Assessment

Have students list some examples of contributions immigrants have brought to the United States over the years. Use this assessment to monitor students' understanding and identify the need for intervention.

netw⊙rks

Go to **connected.mcgraw-hill.com** for additional resources:

• Interactive Whiteboard Lessons
• Worksheets
• Assessment
• Content Library

My family and I went to a Caribbean carnival downtown. It was so colorful! People were dressed in costumes and dancing. Long ago, people in the Caribbean Islands danced through their villages in costumes. Today people enjoy practicing this tradition at carnivals around the world.

I went to the Miami Art Museum with my family. I noticed some paintings that were made by an African American artist named Jacob Lawrence. He was inspired by African art, which typically uses flat shapes and bright colors. He borrowed these ideas and made them a part of his work.

Write down something that you learned from Paula's presentation.

When I was walking home from school last week someone asked if I had seen their missing Chihuahua. I had never heard of a Chihuahua. The person said a Chihuahua is a kind of dog. The name comes from a state in Mexico. This is an example of a Mexican word that we use in our language today.

"Some customs are brought to the United States by immigrants. Other customs are created right here," said Paula. "Together these customs from near and far mix and make one big culture that we all share. In fact, the United States has one of the most diverse cultures on Earth!"

The class clapped for Paula at the end of her presentation. Mrs. Jones told everyone that they had done a wonderful job teaching each other.

Lesson 3

? Essential Question **How does culture shape a community?**

Go back to *Show As You Go!* **on pages 60–61.**

netw*o*rks *There's More Online! Games • Assessment*

86

87

Lesson 3

Active Teaching

Read the pages together to help students understand that the United States has a diverse culture. Guide students through the written activities. Discuss their responses.

Develop Comprehension

Ask:

1. *What are some other examples of art you have seen from different cultures?* **L2**

2. *Why does the United States have one of the most diverse cultures?* **L3**

Summarize the lesson with the class. Then have students respond to the Essential Question. Discuss students' responses. Have students revisit their response on page 80 and compare it to their response at the end of the lesson. Discuss how their answers changed.

Use the leveled reader, *Cuba and the United States,* to extend and enrich students' understanding of Cuban immigrants' contributions to the United States. A lesson plan for this leveled reader can be found on pages T22–T23 at the front of this Teacher Edition.

Show As You Go! Remind students to go back to the Unit Opener and complete the activities for this lesson.

Response to Intervention

? Essential Question **How does culture shape a community?**

If . . . students cannot give a substantiated response to the Essential Question, "How does culture shape a community?"

. . . .

Then . . . take students back to pages 80 through 85. Discuss the ways cultures from different countries have shaped the United States.

Ask: *What are some ways cultures from other countries have shaped the culture in the United States?*

Following the discussion, allow students to respond to the Essential Question again.

More About Jacob Lawrence Lawrence is among the best-known African American painters. His "Migration Series," which depicted the northward movement of African Americans during the Depression, made him nationally famous when it was featured in a 1941 issue of Fortune Magazine. Lawrence's work often focuses on important periods in African American history. Among his works are portrayals of the abolitionist John Brown, the Haitian revolutionary Toussaint L'Ouverture, and Harriet Tubman.

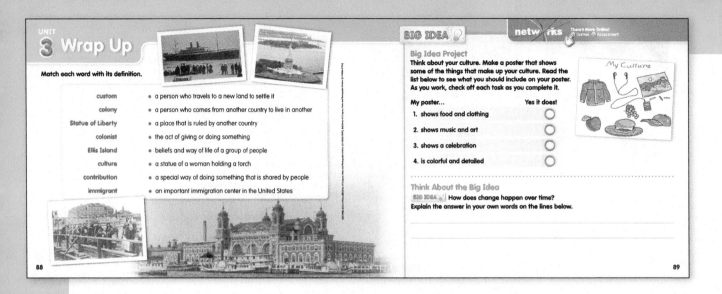

Unit 3 Wrap Up

Matching Have students complete the activity on page 86 to review the Unit vocabulary.

BIG IDEA **Big Idea Project**

Students will be making a poster about their culture to show what they learned in Unit 3.

- Read the checklist together and answer questions students may have about the project.

- Have students cut out pictures from magazines, draw their own pictures, or bring in family pictures to create their posters.

- Have students label and briefly describe each picture on their posters.

- Have students share their posters with the class. Then display the posters in the classroom.

- To assess the project, refer to the rubric on the following page.

Differentiated Instruction

▶ **Approaching** Students can include fewer than five cultural items on their poster. Students may verbally explain what is on their poster.

▶ **Beyond** Have students talk to their parents about additional cultural influences to their family. Have them include one of these on their poster.

▶ **ELL** Have students circle key words from the checklist that they need to include on their posters. Make sure students understand the directions for the project. Students may explain what is on their posters orally rather than in writing.

Response to Intervention

BIG IDEA Change happens over time.

If . . . students cannot give a substantiated response to the Big Idea, "Change happens over time"

Then . . . have students think about the change that occurred in each lesson. Ask students to describe the changes. Point out examples of change in each lesson, for example: How did life in Colonial America change over time? How did immigration change the culture in the United States? Following the discussion, allow students to respond to the Big Idea again.

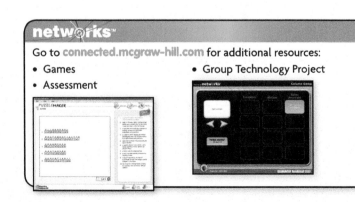

netw rks™

Go to **connected.mcgraw-hill.com** for additional resources:

- Games
- Assessment
- Group Technology Project

Name _____ Date _____

Cultural Poster Rubric

4 Exemplary	3 Accomplished	2 Developing	1 Beginning
The poster: ☐ includes pictures of all cultural elements. ☐ contains accurate labels and descriptions for the cultural elements. ☐ contains few, if any, errors in capitalization and spelling of the names of places.	**The poster:** ☐ includes pictures of most cultural elements. ☐ has mostly accurate labels and descriptions for the cultural elements. ☐ contains some errors in capitalization and spelling of the names of places.	**The poster:** ☐ includes pictures of a few cultural elements. ☐ has some accurate labels and descriptions for the cultural elements. ☐ contains several errors in capitalization and spelling of the names of places.	**The poster:** ☐ includes pictures of at least one cultural element. ☐ has few accurate labels and descriptions for the cultural elements. ☐ contains serious errors in capitalization and spelling of the names of places.

Grading Comments: _____

_____

_____

_____

_____

_____

_____

_____

_____

_____

_____

_____

_____

Project Score: _____

Teacher Notes

Teacher Notes

UNIT
4 Planner CITIZENS AND GOVERNMENT

BIG IDEA 💡 **People's actions affect others.**

Student Portfolio

- ***Show As You Go!***
  Use these pages to introduce the Big Idea. Students record information specific to each lesson. They use these pages to help them plan their Big Idea Project.

net~~w~~orks

- **Group Technology Project**
  Students use 21st century skills to complete a group extension activity of the unit project. Lesson plans, worksheets and rubrics are available online.

Student Portfolio

- **Big Idea Project**
  Students create a mobile to show what they learned about American citizens and government. The Big Idea Project rubric is on page 125W.

Reading Skills

Student Portfolio

- **Reading Skill: Author's Purpose**
  Pages 90–91. Common Core State Standards RI.6, RI.8

net~~w~~orks

- **Skill Builders**
  Introduce and practice the reading skill.

Leveled Readers

Use the leveled reader, *People Helping People After Hurricane Katrina* (lesson plan on pages T24–T25) with Lesson 2; *George Washington Carver: The Plant Doctor* (lesson plan on pages T26–T27) with Lesson 3; and *Carl B. Stokes* (lesson plan on pages T28–T29) with Lesson 4.

Treasures Connection

Teach this unit with Treasures Unit 3, *Officer Buckle and Gloria*, pages 336–360.

Social Studies Skills

Student Portfolio

- **Primary and Secondary Sources: Documents and Audio/Video Recordings**
  Page 95

net~~w~~orks

- **Skill Builders**
  Introduce and teach analyzing primary and secondary sources.

Activity Cards

- **Center for Social Studies Skills Investigation**
  Use the center activity cards to help students explore Primary Sources, Geography, and Citizenship.

FOLDABLES®

Student Portfolio

- Students can create vocabulary Foldables right in their portfolios.

Assessment Solutions

- **McGraw-Hill networks™**
  Safe online testing features multiple question types that are easy to use and editable!

- **Self-Check Quizzes**

- **Worksheets**

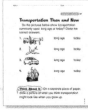

UNIT 4 **At a Glance**

Lesson	Essential Question	Vocabulary	Digital Resources
1 United States Citizens Pages 96–99	What does it mean to belong to a country?	citizen naturalization *introduce	Go to **connected.mcgraw-hill.com** for additional resources: • Interactive Whiteboard Lessons
2 Rights and Responsibilities Pages 100–105	What does it mean to be a citizen?	rights responsible recycle volunteer *positive	• Worksheets • Assessment
3 Citizens Create Change Pages 106–111	How can citizens create change?	veteran *equal	• Lesson Plans
4 Rules and Laws Pages 112–117	How do people get along?	government Constitution *structure *function	• Content Library • Skill Builders
5 American Symbols Pages 118–123	What represents a country?	symbol *represent	• Videos • Use Standards Tracker on **networks** to track students' progress

*denotes academic vocabulary

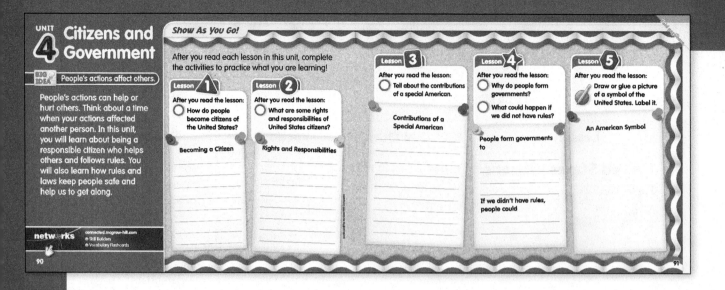

90 91

Introduce the Unit

☑ Diagnostic Assessment

Write the following phrases on sentence strips and tape them to the board:

- take part in a food drive
- recycle glass, plastic, and paper
- take things that do not belong to you
- cross the street at the crosswalk
- push to the front of the line
- throw litter on the ground

Have students read each phrase. Engage students in a discussion about the effects of each action. Then draw a two-column chart on the board. Write *Actions that are Helpful* at the top of one column and *Actions that Hurt Others* at the top of the other. Have students sort each phrase into the appropriate group. Students' responses will help identify their level of understanding.

Say: *In this unit, we will learn more about how people's actions affect others.*

Active Teaching

BIG IDEA People's actions affect others.

In this unit, students will learn how to make their community a better place to live, whether by helping others or by following rules. Students will use the *Show As You Go!* pages throughout their study of this unit. After they read each lesson, students will use information from the lesson to complete these pages.

At this point, have students fold back the corner of this page. This will help them flip back to page 89 as needed. Explain to students that at the end of the unit, they will use the information collected on these pages to complete their Big Idea Project.

Differentiated Instruction

▶ **Approaching** Review the directions with students and help define any unfamiliar words. After each lesson, allow students to work in a small group to complete the activity.

▶ **Beyond** Have students include appropriate capitalization and punctuation in their answers.

▶ **ELL** Have students circle key words in the directions. Define unfamiliar words. As lessons are completed, allow students to work with a partner to discuss and record information on the pages.

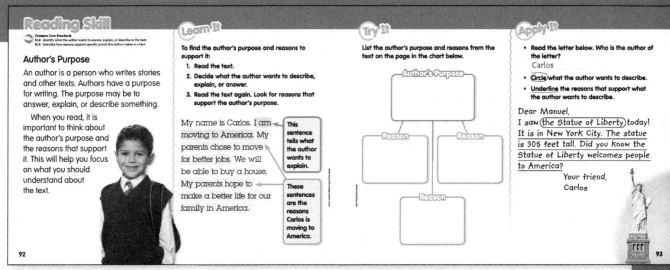

Common Core Standards **RI.6:** Identify what the author wants to answer, explain, or describe in the text. **RI.8:** Describe how reasons support specific points the author makes in a text.

Reading Skill

Active Teaching

(LEARN IT) Author's Purpose

Read the introductory paragraphs and the LEARN IT activity together. Share this active reading strategy for identifying the author's purpose of a text.

Say: *As I read, I keep this question in mind, "What does the author want to explain, answer, or describe?" Once I know the answer, I look for reasons to support it. Identifying the author's purpose and supporting reasons helps me to focus on what the author wants me to know.*

(TRY IT) Encourage students to try the modeled
strategy as they complete the TRY IT activity.

(APPLY IT) Have students complete the APPLY IT
activity.

Ask:

1. *What question should you ask yourself to help identify the author's purpose?* (What is that author explaining, describing, or answering?) **L1**

2. *How do reasons support the author's purpose?* (They give more information about what the author is describing.) **L2**

3. *Why is it important to identify the author's purpose?* **L3**

Differentiated Instruction

▶ **Approaching** Review the LEARN IT activity as a small group. Do the TRY IT activity together. Have students complete the APPLY IT activity independently. Regroup to compare and correct.

▶ **Beyond** Provide a variety of short paragraphs for students to use to determine the author's purpose. Have them complete Author's Purpose and Supporting Reasons graphic organizers for the paragraphs they examine. Have students explain their work to a partner.

▶ **ELL** Explain the words *author* and *purpose* to students. Describe situations where an author would *answer*, *explain*, or *describe* something. Reread the selections on pages 90 and 91 and discuss what the author is answering, explaining, or describing. Then have students identify the sentences that support the author's purpose. Model for students how to complete the graphic organizer.

netw⊙rks

Go to **connected.mcgraw-hill.com** for additional resources:

• Graphic Organizers   • Skill Builders

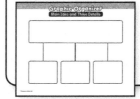

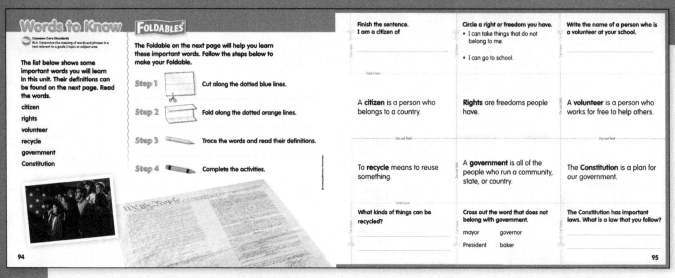

Words to Know — **FOLDABLES**

Common Core Standards
RI.4 Determine the meaning of words and phrases in a text relevant to a grade 2 topic or subject area.

The list below shows some important words you will learn in this unit. Their definitions can be found on the next page. Read the words.

citizen
rights
volunteer
recycle
government
Constitution

The Foldable on the next page will help you learn these important words. Follow the steps below to make your Foldable.

Step 1 Cut along the dotted blue lines.
Step 2 Fold along the dotted orange lines.
Step 3 Trace the words and read their definitions.
Step 4 Complete the activities.

Finish the sentence. I am a citizen of ____

Circle a right or freedom you have.
• I can take things that do not belong to me.
• I can go to school.

Write the name of a person who is a volunteer at your school.

A **citizen** is a person who belongs to a country.

Rights are freedoms people have.

A **volunteer** is a person who works for free to help others.

To **recycle** means to reuse something.

A **government** is all of the people who run a community, state, or country.

The **Constitution** is a plan for our government.

What kinds of things can be recycled?

Cross out the word that does not belong with government.
mayor   governor
President   baker

The Constitution has important laws. What is a law that you follow?

Common Core Standards RI.4: Determine the meaning of words and phrases in a text relevant to a grade 2 topic or subject area.

Words to Know
Active Teaching

 FOLDABLES

1. Go to connected.mcgraw-hill.com for flashcards to introduce the unit vocabulary to students.

2. Read the list on page 92 and have students repeat after you.

3. Then guide students as they complete steps 1 through 4 of the Vocabulary Foldable.

4. Have students use the Vocabulary Foldable to practice the vocabulary independently or with a partner.

networks

Go to connected.mcgraw-hill.com for additional resources:
- Vocabulary Flashcards
- Vocabulary Games
- Graphic Organizers

GO Vocabulary!

Use the graphic organizer below to help students practice the meanings of the words from the list. Model for students how to complete the graphic organizer using the word *veteran*. Have students complete the graphic organizer for the other words independently or with a partner.

A veteran is a person who was a service member in our country's Army, Navy, Air Force, or Marines.

A veteran is a person who fought for and protected our country.

veteran

We honor veterans and consider them heroes.

We celebrate veterans young and old on a holiday called Veteran's Day.

FOLDABLES®

Primary Sources

Documents are a type of primary source. A document is a paper that gives information. The document pictured here is the Constitution of the United States.

Audio and video recordings are also sources of information. They have sound and moving pictures. The video recording pictured here is a secondary source. A secondary source is something that is made or written after an event happens. This video recording is about the Constitution.

DBQ Document-Based Questions

1. **How can you tell the first three words of the Constitution are important?**
   They are larger than the other words.

2. **Why do you think this video recording about the Constitution was made?**

netw⊙rks
There's More Online!
• Skill Builders
• Resource Library

Differentiated Instruction

▶ **ELL** Group the following words together:

citizen – rights

government – Constitution

recycle – volunteer

Say: *How do these words relate to each other?*

Have students help make a list of ways each group of words are connected to each other.

W O R D   P L A Y

Play Vocabulary Baseball:

1. Divide the class into two teams.

2. Push the desks to the sides of the room.

3. Set up four bases.

4. Have the students take turns "at bat." They must give the definition when given the word, state the word when given the definition, or supply the correct word for a sentence.

5. Students may advance to each base if they answer correctly.

Active Teaching

Ask students to describe how the images on page 95 are the same and different. Tell students that the Constitution is a document that lists the most important laws in the United States. Explain to students that the original document was written over two hundred years ago.

Read and discuss page 95 together. Make sure students are clear about the definitions of the words *primary source* and *secondary source*. Guide students through the written activities.

Ask:

1. *Why is the Constitution a primary source?* (It is a document that was written over two hundred years ago.) **L1**

2. *Why is the video recording about the Constitution a secondary source?* (It was made after the Constitution was written.) **L2**

netw⊙rks

Go to connected.mcgraw-hill.com for additional resources:
• Skill Builders
• Resource Library

Activate Prior Knowledge

Look at a political map of the world with the students. Explain to students that people who are born in a country are citizens of that country. Point to several countries and tell students what the citizens who live in each country are called. For example, citizens of the United States are Americans, citizens of Canada are Canadians, citizens of Mexico are Mexicans, etc.

Engage students in a discussion about the country where they were born. Have volunteers point to their birth country on the map.

Ask: *What do you think citizens of Florida are called?*

Explain that in this lesson, they will learn about what it means to belong to a country.

? Essential Question What does it mean to belong to a country?

Have students explain what they understand about the Essential Question. Discuss their responses. Explain that everything they learn in this lesson will help them understand the Essential Question better. Remind them to think about how the Essential Question connects to the unit Big Idea: People's actions affect others.

Active Teaching

Words To Know Have students look through the lesson to find the words that are listed in the Word Hunt. Then have them read the definitions of the content vocabulary words and use context clues or the glossary to determine the meaning of the academic vocabulary word *introduce*. To help students understand the word *introduce*, have groups of three students role-play introducing each other.

Develop Comprehension

Read pages 96 and 97 together. Discuss the ways people become citizens of a country. Take a poll of students who were born in the United States and students who were born in another country. Make a graph to show the results of the poll. Guide students through the written activities and allow them to share their work in small groups.

Ask:

1. *What is a citizen?* (A citizen is a person who belongs to a country.) **L1**

2. *What are the two ways people become citizens of a country?* (birth and naturalization) **L1**

3. *What are some reasons people move to the United States and become naturalized citizens?* **L2**

Differentiated Instruction

▶ **ELL** Draw a concept map graphic organizer and write the title, "Becoming Citizens," at the center. Have students describe the two ways people become citizens in their own words. Record their words on the graphic organizer. Read the graphic organizer together.

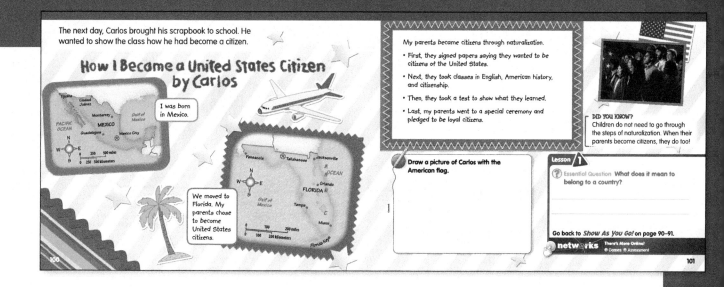

The next day, Carlos brought his scrapbook to school. He wanted to show the class how he had become a citizen.

How I Became a United States Citizen by Carlos

I was born in Mexico.

We moved to Florida. My parents chose to become United States citizens.

My parents became citizens through naturalization.

- First, they signed papers saying they wanted to be citizens of the United States.
- Next, they took classes in English, American history, and citizenship.
- Then, they took a test to show what they learned.
- Last, my parents went to a special ceremony and pledged to be loyal citizens.

DID YOU KNOW?
Children do not need to go through the steps of naturalization. When their parents become citizens, they do too!

Draw a picture of Carlos with the American flag.

Lesson 1

(?) Essential Question What does it mean to belong to a country?

Go back to *Show As You Go!* on page 90–91.

netw⊙rks There's More Online!
⊙ Games ⊙ Assessment

100   101

Active Teaching

Read the pages together to help students learn about the steps of naturalization. Guide students through the written activities, except for the Essential Question.

Ask:

1. *Where was Carlos born?* (in Mexico) **L1**
2. *What are the steps of naturalization?* (sign papers, take classes, take a test, pledge loyalty at a special ceremony) **L2**
3. *How did Carlos become a citizen?* **L3**

Summarize the lesson with the class. Then have students respond to the Essential Question. Discuss their responses. Have students revisit their response on page 96 and compare it to their response at the end of the lesson. Discuss how their answers changed.

> **Show As You Go!** Remind students to go back to the Unit Opener to complete the activities for this lesson.

Response to Intervention

(?) Essential Question **What does it mean to belong to a country?**

If . . . students cannot give a response to the Essential Question, "What does it mean to belong to a country?"

. . . .

Then . . . take students back to pages 96 through 99. Discuss the two ways people become citizens of a country. Following the discussion, allow students to respond to the Essential Question again.

netw⊙rks

Go to connected.mcgraw-hill.com for additional resources:

- Interactive Whiteboard Lessons
- Assessment
- Lesson Plans
- Worksheets

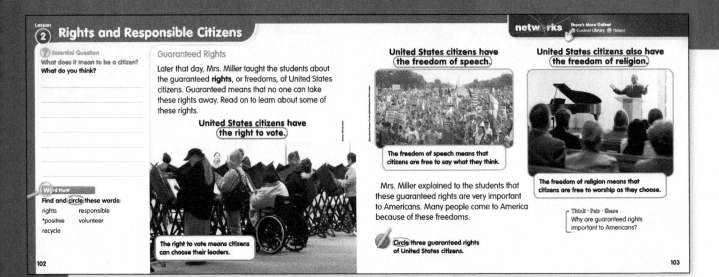

Lesson
(2) **Rights and Responsible Citizens**

net**w**rks | There's More Online!
Content Library ⊕ Videos

? Essential Question
What does it mean to be a citizen?
What do you think?

Guaranteed Rights

Later that day, Mrs. Miller taught the students about the guaranteed **rights**, or freedoms, of United States citizens. Guaranteed means that no one can take these rights away. Read on to learn about some of these rights.

United States citizens have (the right to vote.)

The right to vote means citizens can choose their leaders.

United States citizens have (the freedom of speech.)

The freedom of speech means that citizens are free to say what they think.

Mrs. Miller explained to the students that these guaranteed rights are very important to Americans. Many people come to America because of these freedoms.

🔍 Circle three guaranteed rights of United States citizens.

United States citizens also have (the freedom of religion.)

The freedom of religion means that citizens are free to worship as they choose.

┌ Think · Pair · Share
│ Why are guaranteed rights
│ important to Americans?

Word Hunt
Find and circle these words:
rights   responsible
*positive   volunteer
recycle

102   103

Lesson 2

Activate Prior Knowledge

Have students complete the following sentence:
As a United States citizen, I can _____.
Record and discuss their responses. Tell students that in this lesson, they will learn more about the rights and responsibilities they have as United States citizens.

? **Essential Question What does it mean to be a citizen?**

Have students explain what they understand about the Essential Question. Discuss their responses. Explain that everything they learn in this lesson will help them understand the Essential Question better. Remind them to think about how the Essential Question connects to the unit Big Idea: People's actions affect others.

Active Teaching

Words To Know Have students look through the lesson to find the words that are listed in the Word Hunt. Then have them read the definitions of the content vocabulary words and use context clues or the glossary to determine the meaning of the academic vocabulary word *positive*. Next tell students that they will learn how citizens can have a positive, or good, effect in their community.

Develop Comprehension

Discuss the pictures and the headings on pages 100 and 101. After reading together, have pairs engage in the Think Pair Share activity. Ask students to share what they discussed.

Ask:

1. *What does it mean that the rights of United States citizens are guaranteed?* (It means that these rights cannot be taken away.) **L1**

2. *What are some of the guaranteed rights we have as United States citizens?* (the right to vote, the freedom of religion, and the freedom of speech) **L2**

3. *Why do you think guaranteed rights are reasons people move to the United States?* **L3**

Differentiated Instruction

▶ **ELL** To help students understand the word *rights*, have them list the things they have the freedom to do, for example, go to school, ride their bikes, or eat meals with their family. Discuss their responses.

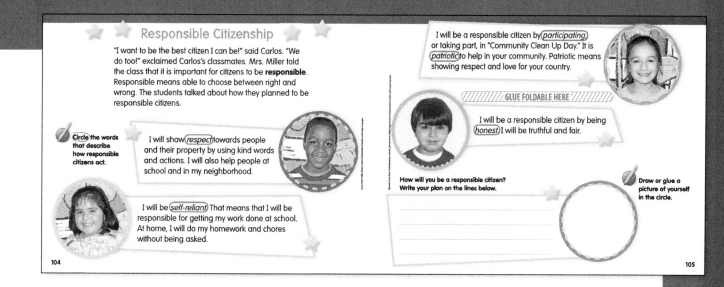

Responsible Citizenship

"I want to be the best citizen I can be!" said Carlos. "We do too!" exclaimed Carlos's classmates. Mrs. Miller told the class that it is important for citizens to be **responsible**. Responsible means able to choose between right and wrong. The students talked about how they planned to be responsible citizens.

Circle the words that describe how responsible citizens act.

I will show respect towards people and their property by using kind words and actions. I will also help people at school and in my neighborhood.

I will be self-reliant. That means that I will be responsible for getting my work done at school. At home, I will do my homework and chores without being asked.

I will be a responsible citizen by participating, or taking part, in "Community Clean Up Day." It is patriotic to help in your community. Patriotic means showing respect and love for your country.

////// GLUE FOLDABLE HERE //////

I will be a responsible citizen by being honest. I will be truthful and fair.

How will you be a responsible citizen? Write your plan on the lines below.

_____

_____

_____

Draw or glue a picture of yourself in the circle.

104

105

Active Teaching

Tell students that good citizens display characteristics of responsible citizenship. Read about the characteristics on pages 102 and 103 together. Have students write how they plan to be responsible citizens. Have them share their plans in small groups.

Develop Comprehension

Ask:

1. *What does the word* responsible *mean?* (able to choose between right and wrong) **L1**

2. *How can you be a responsible citizen?* (by being respectful, self-reliant, patriotic, honest, and by participating in making the community a better place) **L2**

3. *Why is it important to be a responsible citizen?* **L3**

Use the leveled reader, *People Helping People: After Hurricane Katrina,* to extend and enrich students' understanding of responsible citizenship. A lesson plan for this leveled reader can be found on pages T24–T25 at the front of this Teacher Edition.

☑ Formative Assessment

Have students list the characteristics of a responsible citizen. Then have students role play the application of each characteristic. Use this assessment to monitor students' understanding and identify the need for intervention.

Differentiated Instruction

▶ **Approaching** Have students list the characteristics of responsible citizenship on the board. Describe various scenarios and have students tell how they will apply each characteristic.

▶ **Beyond** Have students write and act in several skits showing how they will apply the characteristics of responsible citizenship. Have students perform the skits for the class.

▶ **ELL** List the characteristics of responsible citizenship on the board and read them together. Paraphrase the meaning of each characteristic for students. Have students orally complete the following sentence frame with each characteristic:

I will be _____ by _____.

Page Power

FOLDABLES Interact more with the page. Have students create a Notebook Foldable to assist them in developing their understanding of the characteristics of responsible citizenship.

1. Provide each student with a copy of Foldable 4A from the Notebook Foldables section at the back of this book.

2. Have students construct the Foldable and glue its anchor tab above their responsible citizenship plan on page 103.

3. On the outside Foldable flap, have students draw a picture of themselves being responsible citizens.

4. Under the flap, have students write the characteristics that they are applying.

"Responsible citizens also make contributions to make our country a better place to live," said Mrs. Miller. A contribution is something a person does to help others. One way citizens can make a **positive** contribution to the community is by being a **volunteer** in the community. A volunteer is a person who works for free to help others. How are the volunteers in these pictures helping others?

Write a caption for each picture.

"I know another way we can help our environment!" said Lin. "We can **recycle**!" To recycle means to reuse something. Glass, plastic, and newspapers can be recycled and made into something else. Recycling helps protect our environment.

What is another way to make a positive contribution to your community?

_____

_____

Draw a picture that shows something you can do to make a positive change to your environment.

Lesson **2**

? Essential Question What does it mean to be a citizen?

_____

_____

Go back to *Show As You Go!* on pages 90–91.

netw⊕rks There's More Online!
⊕ Games ⊕ Assessment

106

107

Lesson 2

Active Teaching

Discuss the pictures on pages 104 and 105. As students read, have them think about how they can make a positive contribution to their community. Read and discuss the pages together. Guide students through the written activities, except for the Essential Question. Discuss the captions students wrote for each picture.

Develop Comprehension

Ask:

1. *How do volunteers make positive contributions to the community?* (Volunteers work for free to help people in their community.) **L1**

2. *Why is recycling a way to make a positive contribution to the community?* **L2**

3. *Why is it important for citizens to contribute to their community?* **L3**

Summarize the lesson with the class. Then have students respond to the Essential Question. Discuss students' responses. Have students revisit their response on page 100 and compare it to their response at the end of the lesson. Discuss how their answers changed.

> *Show As You Go!* Remind students to go back to the Unit Opener to complete the activities for this lesson.

Response to Intervention

? Essential Question **What does it mean to be a citizen?**

If... students cannot give a response to the Essential Question, "What does it mean to be a citizen?"

· ·

Then... review the story about Carlos from Lesson 2. Ask students what Carlos learned about the guaranteed rights and responsibilities of United States citizens. List their answers on the board. Discuss that the rights and responsibilities are part of what it means to be a citizen. Following the discussion, allow students to respond to the Essential Question again.

netw⊕rks

Go to **connected.mcgraw-hill.com** for additional resources:

- Interactive Whiteboard Lessons
- Worksheets
- Assessment
- Lesson Plans
- Content Library

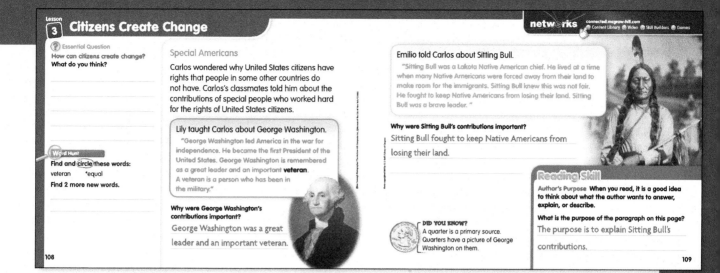

Essential Question
How can citizens create change?
What do you think?

Word Hunt
Find and circle these words:
veteran   *equal
Find 2 more new words.

Special Americans

Carlos wondered why United States citizens have rights that people in some other countries do not have. Carlos's classmates told him about the contributions of special people who worked hard for the rights of United States citizens.

Lily taught Carlos about George Washington.

"George Washington led America in the war for independence. He became the first President of the United States. George Washington is remembered as a great leader and an important **veteran**. A veteran is a person who has been in the military."

Why were George Washington's contributions important?

George Washington was a great leader and an important veteran.

108

Emilio told Carlos about Sitting Bull.

"Sitting Bull was a Lakota Native American chief. He lived at a time when many Native Americans were forced away from their land to make room for the immigrants. Sitting Bull knew this was not fair. He fought to keep Native Americans from losing their land. Sitting Bull was a brave leader."

Why were Sitting Bull's contributions important?

Sitting Bull fought to keep Native Americans from losing their land.

DID YOU KNOW?
A quarter is a primary source. Quarters have a picture of George Washington on them.

Reading Skill

Author's Purpose When you read, it is a good idea to think about what the author wants to answer, explain, or describe.

What is the purpose of the paragraph on this page?

The purpose is to explain Sitting Bull's contributions.

109

Lesson 3

Activate Prior Knowledge

Remind students that today all United States citizens have guaranteed rights. Tell students that long ago in the United States, some Americans did not have the same freedoms. Explain that some people were treated unfairly.

Ask: *What would you do if you saw that someone was being treated unfairly?*

Say: *In this lesson, you will learn about special people who worked hard for the rights of American citizens.*

? Essential Question How can citizens create change?

Have students explain what they understand about the Essential Question. Discuss their responses. Explain that everything they learn in this lesson will help them understand the Essential Question better. Remind them to think about how the Essential Question connects to the unit Big Idea: People's actions affect others.

Reading Skill

 Common Core Standards RI.2.6: Identify what the author wants to answer, explain, or describe in the text.

Author's Purpose For additional practice, have students determine what the author is explaining, describing, or answering in the other paragraphs.

Active Teaching

Words To Know Have students look through the lesson to find the words that are listed in the Word Hunt. Define the academic vocabulary word *equal* for students. Ask students to talk about an experiences at home or at school when they were or were not treated equally.

Develop Comprehension

As students read about the people in the lesson, have them think about how each person fought for the rights of American citizens. Read pages 106 and 107 together. Have students evaluate George Washington and Sitting Bull's contributions. Discuss their responses.

Ask:

1. *How did George Washington create change?* (He led America in the war for independence.) **L2**

2. *What was unfair in Sitting Bull's time?* (Native Americans were forced off their land.) **L2**

3. *How were George Washington and Sitting Bull the same and different?* **L3**

Differentiated Instruction

▶ **ELL** Help students understand the words *fair*, *unfair*, and *equal rights*. Divide the students in to two groups. Allow only one group to get a drink of water. Discuss that it was *unfair* that only one group got a drink. Explain that it would be *fair* for the other group to also get a drink of water. Allow the other students to get a drink of water. Discuss that equal rights means that everyone should be treated the same.

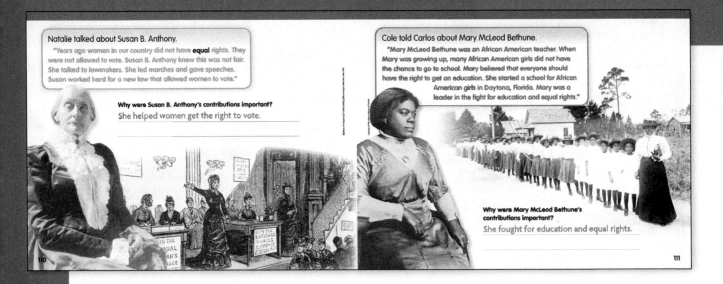

Natalie talked about Susan B. Anthony.

"Years ago women in our country did not have **equal** rights. They were not allowed to vote. Susan B. Anthony knew this was not fair. She talked to lawmakers. She led marches and gave speeches. Susan worked hard for a new law that allowed women to vote."

Why were Susan B. Anthony's contributions important?
She helped women get the right to vote.

Cole told Carlos about Mary McLeod Bethune.

"Mary McLeod Bethune was an African American teacher. When Mary was growing up, many African American girls did not have the chance to go to school. Mary believed that everyone should have the right to get an education. She started a school for African American girls in Daytona, Florida. Mary was a leader in the fight for education and equal rights."

Why were Mary McLeod Bethune's contributions important?
She fought for education and equal rights.

110   111

Lesson 3

Active Teaching

Read about the contributions of Susan B. Anthony and Mary McLeod Bethune on pages 108 and 109. Have students evaluate each person's contributions. Discuss their responses.

Develop Comprehension

Ask:

1. *How was life for Susan B. Anthony different than life in the United States today?* (Women were not allowed to vote.) **L2**

2. *What was unfair during Mary McLeod Bethune's time?* (African American girls did not have the chance to go to school.) **L2**

3. *How did Susan B. Anthony and Mary McLeod Bethune create change?* **L3**

Use the leveled reader, *George Washington Carver: The Plant Doctor,* to extend and enrich students' understanding of how people create change. A lesson plan for this leveled reader can be found on pages T26–T27 at the front of this Teacher Edition.

✓ Formative Assessment

List each person and their contributions on separate index cards. Have students match each person to their contributions. Then have students explain why each contribution was important to our country. Use this assessment to monitor students' understanding and identify the need for intervention.

Differentiated Instruction

▶ **Approaching** Reread the paragraphs about Susan B. Anthony and Mary McLeod Bethune with students. After each paragraph, discuss each person's contributions. Then have students explain why their contributions were important.

▶ **Beyond** Have students make a three-column chart. Head the columns with the words *Person, Contribution,* and *Why the Contribution Was Important.* Have students list each person from the lesson, their contributions, and the value of their contributions.

▶ **ELL** Create concept maps about the people in the lesson. Complete the concept maps with information about each person. Then have students use the information from the concept maps to tell why each person's contribution was important.

Sean taught Carlos about Dr. Martin Luther King, Jr.

"Dr. Martin Luther King, Jr., believed that everyone should be treated the same. He made speeches and led peaceful marches to help change unfair laws. Dr. Martin Luther King, Jr., led the fight for equal rights for all Americans."

Why were Dr. Martin Luther King, Jr.'s, contributions important?
He led the fight for equal rights for all Americans.

Lin told Carlos about Rosa Parks.

"Years ago, many states had unfair laws. One law was that African Americans had to give up their seats to white people on crowded buses. Rosa Parks refused to give up her seat. Police took her to jail. Dr. Martin Luther King, Jr., helped Rosa. He asked people to stop riding buses. People listened. Finally, the law was changed."

Why were Rosa Park's contributions important?
She helped change an unfair law.

112

Ben taught Carlos about César Chávez.

"César Chávez was a famous Hispanic leader. He worked to make life better for farm workers. Laws said that farm workers did not have to be treated the same as other workers. They had to work long hours and were paid very little money. César Chávez gave speeches and led marches to change these laws. His actions helped farm workers to have more rights."

Why were César Chávez's contributions important?
He worked to make life better for farm workers.

Media Center

Use the Internet and other sources to find out:

1. What is the name of the speech Dr. Martin Luther King, Jr., made on August 28, 1963?
   "I Have a Dream"

2. When did Susan B. Anthony and other women in the United States get the right to vote?
   1920

Lesson 3

(?) **Essential Question** How can citizens create change?

Go back to *Show As You Go!* on pages 90–91.

networks There's More Online!
• Games • Assessment

113

Active Teaching

As students read, have them think about how Martin Luther King, Jr., Rosa Parks, and César Chávez worked for people's rights. Guide students as they complete the written activities, except for the Essential Question. Discuss their responses.

Develop Comprehension

Ask:

1. *How did Martin Luther King, Jr., Rosa Parks, and César Chávez bring about change?* **L2**

2. *What freedoms do we enjoy today because of the contributions of the people in this lesson?* **L2**

3. *How are the people in this lesson the same? How are they different?* **L3**

Have students visit the Media Center. Assign partners to find the answers to the questions on page 111.

Summarize the lesson with the class. Then have students respond to the Essential Question. Discuss students' responses. Have students revisit their response on page 106 and compare it to their response at the end of the lesson. Discuss how their answers changed.

> ***Show As You Go!*** Remind students to go back to the Unit Opener to complete the activities for this lesson.

Response to Intervention

(?) **Essential Question** How can citizens create change?

If . . . students cannot give a response to the Essential Question, "How can citizens create change?"

. . . .

Then . . . write the name of each person from Lesson 3 in each row of a chart. Discuss with students the contributions of each person and why the contributions were important. Write students' responses on the chart. Discuss how the contributions are similar. Help students make a generalization about the ways citizens can create change. Following the discussion, allow students to respond to the Essential Question again.

networks

Go to **connected.mcgraw-hill.com** for additional resources:

• Interactive Whiteboard Lessons

• Worksheets
• Assessment
• Lesson Plans

Lesson 4 Rules and Laws

networks There's More Online!
Content Library Videos

We Need Rules

Essential Question
How do people get along?
What do you think?

The next day the students explained their classroom rules to Carlos. The students talked about what would happen if they did not follow each rule.

The students agreed that rules are important. Rules at home and at school keep people safe. Rules also help people to be good citizens. Without rules, things would be out of control and people could get hurt.

GLUE FOLDABLE HERE

Word Hunt
Find and circle these words:
government   Constitution
*structure   *function

1. What is a rule that you have in your home or classroom?

2. What would happen if there is a difference of opinion on a rule?

THINK · PAIR · SHARE
The students made a chart to show their classroom rules. Look at the chart below. Write what you think would happen if students did not follow each rule.

Our Classroom Rules		
Classroom Rule	Reason we have this rule:	What would happen if students did not follow this rule?
1. Raise your hand and wait to be called on before speaking out.	This rule helps everyone get a chance to speak in class.	
2. Keep hands, feet, and objects to yourself.	This rule helps keep students safe.	
3. Walk in the classroom and school building. Do not run!	This rule helps keep students, teachers, and visitors safe.	

114

115

Lesson 4

Activate Prior Knowledge

Engage the class in a discussion about having a new student come to the class.

Ask: *If a new student came to our class, what would he or she need to know?*

List students' responses on the board. Guide students in a discussion about why a new student would need to know the classroom rules.

Say: *In this lesson, we will learn why rules, laws, and government are important.*

Essential Question How do people get along?

Have students explain what they understand about the Essential Question. Discuss their responses. Explain that everything they learn in this lesson will help them understand the Essential Question better. Remind them to think about how the Essential Question connects to the unit Big Idea: People's actions affect others.

Page Power

FOLDABLES® Interact more with the page. Have students create a Notebook Foldable to assist them in developing their understanding of the necessity of rules.

1. Provide each student with a copy of Foldable 4B from the Notebook Foldables section at the back of this book.

2. Have students construct the Foldable and glue its anchor tab above the questions on page 112.

3. On the Foldable flaps, have students write their classroom rules.

4. Under the Foldable flaps, have students write why the rules are important.

Active Teaching

Words To Know Have students look through the lesson to find the words that are listed in the Word Hunt. Then have them read the definitions of the words *government* and *Constitution*. Next ask students to name people they know who are part of our government. Then define the academic vocabulary words *structure* and *function*.

Say: *By setting up the structure and function of our government, the Constitution of the United States tells us what our government can or cannot do.*

Develop Comprehension

Read and discuss the importance of rules. Have students write about a rule in their home or school. Discuss their responses. Then have students share what they discussed during the Think Pair Share activity.

Ask:

1. *What are your classroom rules?* **L2**

2. *What could happen if we did not have these rules?* **L2**

3. *Why do we need rules?* **L3**

Our Government

"Rules in a community are called laws," said Mrs. Miller. "Laws are created by our **government**. A government is all of the people who run a community, state, or country. Our government writes laws to keep order and to keep citizens safe. Without laws, people could get hurt."

THINK • PAIR • SHARE
What could happen if we did not have laws in our community?

"Our government also provides many services," said Mrs. Miller. "Police and fire protection are government services. Other services include health programs and schools. People form governments to make life better for citizens."

Circle the sentences that tell why people form governments.

Read the laws that go with each picture. Write a caption for each that tells why the law is important.

Wear a seatbelt in a moving car.

Keep your dog on a leash.

Cross the street at the crosswalk.

116   117

Active Teaching

Read and discuss pages 114 and 115 together to help students learn about the importance of government. Guide students through the written activities. Discuss their responses.

Develop Comprehension

Ask:

1. *Why does our government write laws?* (to keep order and to keep citizens safe) **L1**

2. *How does our government make life better for United States citizens?* (The government writes laws and provides services for citizens.) **L1**

3. *Why do we need government?* **L3**

Use the leveled reader, *Carl B. Stokes*, to extend and enrich students' understanding of how leaders in our government make life better for citizens. A lesson plan for this leveled reader can be found on pages T28–T29 at the front of this Teacher Edition.

☑ Formative Assessment

Have students write what they learned about the importance of rules and government. Use this assessment to monitor students' understanding and identify the need for intervention.

Differentiated Instruction

▶ Approaching Reread the paragraphs about the government. Ask students to find details about the government in the text. Write the details on the board and read them together.

▶ Beyond Have students make a concept map about government. Have them list the purposes of government on the spokes of the concept map.

▶ ELL Write the following words on the board: *laws*, *safe*, and *services*. Make sure students understand the words. Have students finish the following sentences with one of the words:

The government writes _____.

Laws keep people _____.

The government supplies _____ like police and fire protection.

Read the sentences together.

networks

Go to connected.mcgraw-hill.com for additional resources:

- Interactive Whiteboard Lessons
- Worksheets
- Assessment
- Videos

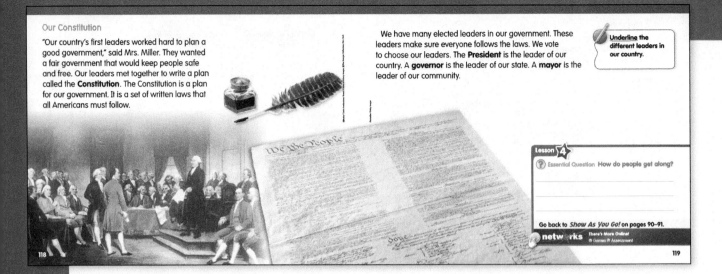

Our Constitution

"Our country's first leaders worked hard to plan a good government," said Mrs. Miller. They wanted a fair government that would keep people safe and free. Our leaders met together to write a plan called the **Constitution**. The Constitution is a plan for our government. It is a set of written laws that all Americans must follow.

We have many elected leaders in our government. These leaders make sure everyone follows the laws. We vote to choose our leaders. The **President** is the leader of our country. A **governor** is the leader of our state. A **mayor** is the leader of our community.

Underline the different leaders in our country.

Lesson 4

? Essential Question How do people get along?

Go back to *Show As You Go!* on pages 90–91.

netw⊕rks There's More Online! Games & Assessment

118   119

Lesson 4

Active Teaching

Have students discuss the images on pages 116 and 117. Read about the Constitution together. Guide students as they complete the written activities, except for the Essential Question. Discuss their responses.

Develop Comprehension

Ask:

1. *What is the Constitution?* (a plan for our government) **L1**

2. *What is the purpose of the Constitution?* (It tells us how our country should be run.) **L2**

3. *Why does the Constitution tell us what our government can and cannot do?* **L3**

Summarize the lesson with the class. Then have students respond to the Essential Question. Have students revisit their response on page 112 and compare it to their response at the end of the lesson. Discuss how their answers changed.

> ***Show As You Go!*** Remind students to go back to the Unit Opener to complete the activities for this lesson.

Response to Intervention

? **Essential Question How do people get along?**

If... students cannot give a response to the Essential Question, "How do people get along?"

....

Then... revisit pages 112 through 117. Discuss how rules, the government, and the Constitution keep people safe and help them get along. Following the discussion, allow students to respond to the Essential Question again.

netw⊕rks

Go to **connected.mcgraw-hill.com** for additional resources:

- Interactive Whiteboard Lessons
- Worksheets
- Assessment
- Lesson Plans

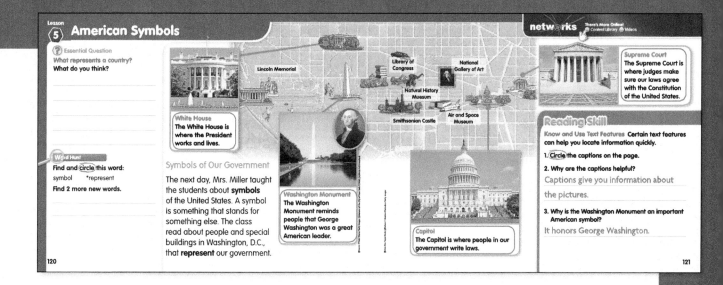

Lesson
5 **American Symbols**

networks There's More Online!
Content Library Videos

Essential Question
What represents a country?
What do you think?

Word Hunt
Find and circle this word:
symbol   *represent
Find 2 more new words.

Lincoln Memorial

White House
The White House is where the President works and lives.

Symbols of Our Government

The next day, Mrs. Miller taught the students about **symbols** of the United States. A symbol is something that stands for something else. The class read about people and special buildings in Washington, D.C., that **represent** our government.

Washington Monument
The Washington Monument reminds people that George Washington was a great American leader.

Library of Congress

National Gallery of Art

Natural History Museum

Smithsonian Castle

Air and Space Museum

Capitol
The Capitol is where people in our government write laws.

Supreme Court
The Supreme Court is where judges make sure our laws agree with the Constitution of the United States.

Reading Skill
Know and Use Text Features Certain text features can help you locate information quickly.
1. Circle the captions on the page.
2. Why are the captions helpful?
Captions give you information about the pictures.
3. Why is the Washington Monument an important American symbol?
It honors George Washington.

120   121

Lesson 5

Activate Prior Knowledge

Play a game to gauge students' prior knowledge.

Say: *Stand up when you see a picture of something that stands for the United States. Sit down if the picture does not stand for the United States.*

Display pictures of various objects and symbols, such as the Constitution, a palm tree, the White House, the moon, the Statue of Liberty, a blue jay, the Liberty Bell, an ocean view, and a Fourth of July parade. Students' responses will help determine their level of understanding.

Explain to students that in this lesson, they will be learning about symbols, people, and events that represent the United States.

Essential Question What represents a country?

Have students explain what they understand about the Essential Question. Discuss their responses. Explain that everything they learn in this lesson will help them understand the Essential Question better. Remind them to think about how the Essential Question connects to the unit Big Idea: People's actions affect others.

Reading Skill

Common Core Standards RI.3: Describe the connection between a series of historical events, scientific ideas or concepts, or steps in technical procedures in a text.

Know and Use Captions For additional practice, ask students to find and circle other captions throughout the lesson.

Active Teaching

Words To Know Have students look through the lesson to find the words that are listed in the Word Hunt. Have them read the definitions of the content vocabulary words and use context clues or the glossary to determine the meaning of the academic vocabulary word *represent*. Next, demonstrate gestures that represent concepts, such as *peace*, *quiet*, or *stop*. Tell students that the gestures are symbols because they represent something else.

Develop Comprehension

Ask students if they have ever visited our country's capital, Washington, D.C.

Ask: *What did you see on your visit?*

Read and discuss the special buildings on pages 118 and 119 together. Guide students through the written activities. Discuss their responses.

Ask:

1. *What is a symbol?* (a picture or thing that stands for something else) **L1**

2. *What symbols of the United States are located in Washington, D.C.?* (the Capitol, the White House, the Supreme Court, and the Washington Monument) **L1**

3. *Why are the buildings on pages 118 and 119 symbols of the United States?* **L2**

Differentiated Instruction

▶ **ELL** Show students pictures of a musical note, a heart, a recycling sign, and the hospital sign. Ask students to tell what each symbol stands for, or represents.

Symbols of Freedom

"Some American symbols stand for freedom," said Mrs. Miller. She told the students about an event called the Fourth of July and a special bell called the Liberty Bell.

Fourth of July The Fourth of July is also known as Independence Day. On this day, we celebrate America's independence, or freedom, from England. People celebrate the event with picnics, parades, and fireworks.

Liberty Bell The Liberty Bell was created to proclaim liberty, or freedom, throughout the land. It is located in Philadelphia, Pennsylvania. The Liberty Bell cannot be rung because it has a crack and might break. But each year on the Fourth of July, it is gently tapped to celebrate America's independence.

DID YOU KNOW? This stamp of the Liberty Bell is a primary source.

Reading Skill

Ask and Answer Questions about Key Details One thing you should do when you read is ask and answer questions about the text.

1. What do Americans celebrate on the Fourth of July? Circle the sentence in the text.

2. What does the word *liberty* mean?
Liberty means freedom.

3. Write your own question about a symbol of the United States. Have a friend answer it.

123

Lesson 5

Active Teaching

Discuss the pictures on pages 120 and 121. Have students tell what they know about the Fourth of July and the Liberty Bell. Read and discuss the pages together. Guide students through the written activities. Discuss their responses.

Ask:

1. *Why does the Fourth of July stand for the United States?* (It is the day we celebrate the birth of the United States.) **L1**

2. *Why is the Liberty Bell a symbol of the United States?* (It stands for the freedom we have in the United States.) **L2**

3. *Why is liberty, or freedom, important to Americans?* **L3**

DID YOU KNOW?

Discuss why students think that the Liberty Bell would be pictured on a stamp.

✔ Formative Assessment

Write the names of various objects and symbols on the board, such as *Constitution, palm trees, White House, moon, blue jay, Liberty Bell, ocean,* and *Fourth of July*. Have students circle the words that name symbols of the United States. Use the assessment to monitor students' understanding and identify the need for intervention.

Differentiated Instruction

▶ **Approaching** Reread the paragraph about the Fourth of July with students. Have students recall key points from the paragraph. Record their answers and read them together. Repeat with the paragraph about the Liberty Bell.

▶ **Beyond** Have students read more about our nation's symbols in the Content Library at connected.mcgraw-hill.com and in trade books. Have students record interesting facts about each symbol and share them with the class.

▶ **ELL** Show students the Fourth of July on a calendar. Explain the meanings of the words *holiday, celebrate,* and *independence*. Explain that the Fourth of July is an important holiday in the United States in which we celebrate the birth of our country. Explain that the Liberty Bell also reminds Americans of independence, or freedom.

Reading Skill

Common Core Standards RI.1: Ask and answer such questions as *who, what, where, when, why,* and *how* to demonstrate understanding of key details in a text.

Ask and Answer Questions about Key Details For additional practice, have students think of other *who, what, where, when, why,* and *how* questions about the text as they read the lesson. Have them read to find the answers.

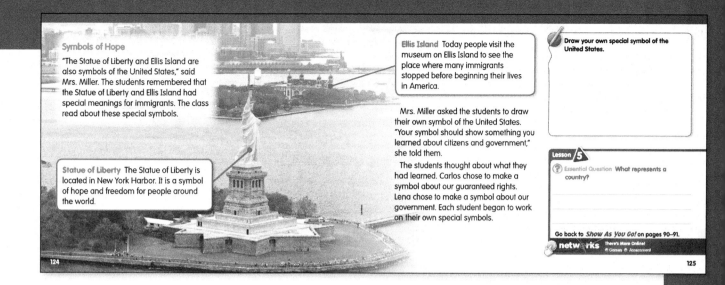

Symbols of Hope

"The Statue of Liberty and Ellis Island are also symbols of the United States," said Mrs. Miller. The students remembered that the Statue of Liberty and Ellis Island had special meanings for immigrants. The class read about these special symbols.

Statue of Liberty The Statue of Liberty is located in New York Harbor. It is a symbol of hope and freedom for people around the world.

Ellis Island Today people visit the museum on Ellis Island to see the place where many immigrants stopped before beginning their lives in America.

Mrs. Miller asked the students to draw their own symbol of the United States. "Your symbol should show something you learned about citizens and government," she told them.

The students thought about what they had learned. Carlos chose to make a symbol about our guaranteed rights. Lena chose to make a symbol about our government. Each student began to work on their own special symbols.

Draw your own special symbol of the United States.

Lesson **5**

Essential Question What represents a country?

Go back to *Show As You Go!* on pages 90–91.

netw**o**rks There's More Online!
⊕ Games ⊕ Assessment

124   125

Active Teaching

Have students tell what they remember about the Statue of Liberty and Ellis Island from Unit 3. Have a discussion about why these things are symbols of the United States. Read the pages together. Guide students as they complete the written activities, except for the Essential Question. Have each student explain the symbol they created.

Develop Comprehension

Ask:

1. *Why are the Statue of Liberty and Ellis Island important symbols of the United States?* (They both stand for the freedoms we have in the United States.) **L2**

2. *How do you think Americans should act when they see a symbol of our country?* **L3**

3. *Why do some people, events, symbols, and documents stand for our country while others do not?* **L3**

Summarize the lesson with the class. Then have students respond to the Essential Question. Discuss their responses. Have students revisit their response on page 118 and compare it to their response at the end of the lesson. Discuss how their answers changed.

Show As You Go! Remind students to go back to complete the project on the Unit Opener.

Response to Intervention

(?) Essential Question What represents a country?

If . . . students cannot give a response to the Essential Question, "What represents a country?"

. . . .

Then . . . have students look through Lesson 5 and name each symbol. List their answers on the board. Then have them take turns completing the following sentence: _____ *stands for our country because* _____.

. . . .

Following the discussion, allow students to respond to the Essential Question again.

netw**o**rks

Go to connected.mcgraw-hill.com for additional resources:

- Interactive Whiteboard Lessons
- Worksheets
- Assessment
- Content Library

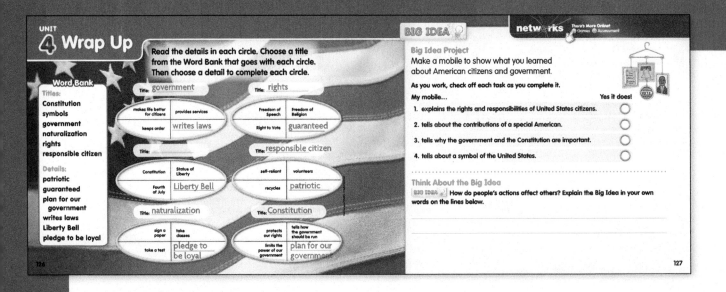

Unit 4 Wrap Up

Concept Circles

Have students read the titles and details in the Word Bank. Then have groups choose titles for each circle and fill in the missing details.

BIG IDEA 🔑 **Big Idea Project**

Students will be making a mobile to show what they learned in Unit 4.

- Read the checklist together and answer students' questions about the project.
- Have students revisit the *Show as You Go* pages for information from each lesson. Provide supplies such as index cards, yarn, and wire coat hangers.
- Have students share their mobiles with the class.
- Then hang the mobiles in the classroom to remind students of what they learned about citizenship and government.
- After students complete their projects, encourage self-reflection by asking:
  1. *How did you plan your mobile?*
  2. *What changes would you make to your project if you did it again?*
- To assess the project, refer to the rubric on the following page.

netw🌐rks

Go to connected.mcgraw-hill.com for additional resources:
- Games
- Group Technology Project
- Assessment

Differentiated Instruction

▶ **Approaching** After students draw pictures for each item on the checklist, have them describe their pictures as you write their words. Read each card together. Allow students who have trouble tying to tape the yarn to the index cards and hanger.

▶ **Beyond** Have students write a paragraph for each item of their mobiles. Their sentences should have correct capitalization and punctuation.

▶ **ELL** Write the following headings on the chalkboard and have students write them on their index cards: *Citizens; Rights and Responsible Citizens; Special Americans; Rules, Laws, and Government; Our Constitution;* and *Symbols.* Have students describe what they will draw and write for each heading before they do the activity.

Response to Intervention

BIG IDEA 🔑 **People's actions affect others.**

If . . . students cannot give a substantiated response to the Big Idea, "People's actions affect others,"
. . . .

Then . . . write several phrases that describe actions discussed in the unit. Have students sort the actions into two groups, *actions that are helpful* and *actions that could hurt others.* Then have students describe the effects of each action with a partner. Following the discussion, allow students to respond to the Big Idea again.

Name _____ Date _____

Citizens and Government Mobile Rubric

4 Exemplary	3 Accomplished	2 Developing	1 Beginning
The mobile:	**The mobile:**	**The mobile:**	**The mobile:**
☐ includes pictures of all checklist items	☐ includes pictures of most checklist items	☐ includes pictures of a few checklist items	☐ includes pictures of at least one checklist item
☐ contains accurate labels and descriptions for each item	☐ has mostly accurate labels and descriptions for each item	☐ has some accurate labels and descriptions for each item	☐ has few accurate labels and descriptions for each item
☐ contains few, if any, errors in capitalization and spelling	☐ contains some errors in capitalization and spelling	☐ contains several errors in capitalization and spelling	☐ contains serious errors in capitalization and spelling

Grading Comments: _____

_____

_____

_____

_____

_____

_____

_____

_____

_____

_____

_____

_____

Project Score: _____

5 Planner ALL ABOUT ECONOMICS

BIG IDEA  **Relationships affect choices.**

Student Portfolio

- ***Show As You Go!***
  Use these pages to introduce the Big Idea. Students record information specific to each lesson. They use these pages to help them plan their Big Idea Project.

networks

- **Group Technology Project**
  Students use 21st century skills to complete a group extension activity of the unit project. Lesson plans, worksheets and rubrics are available online.

Student Portfolio

- **Big Idea Project**
  Students plan and create a picture book to show what they learned about economics. The Big Idea Project rubric is on page 149W.

Reading Skills

Student Portfolio

- **Reading Skill: Cause and Effect**
  Pages 128–129. Common Core State Standards RI.3

networks

- **Skill Builders**
  Introduce and practice the reading skill.

Leveled Readers

Use the leveled reader, *From the Farm*, (lesson plan on pages T30–T31) with Lesson 1.

Treasures Connection

Teach this unit with Treasures Unit 2, *A Trip to the Emergency Room*, pages 222–225.

Social Studies Skills

Student Portfolio

- **Primary Sources: Newspapers**
  Page 133

networks

- **Skill Builders**
  Introduce and teach analyzing primary and secondary sources.

Activity Cards

- **Center for Social Studies Skills Investigation**
  Use the center activity cards to help students explore Primary Sources, Geography, and Citizenship.

FOLDABLES

Student Portfolio

- Students can create vocabulary Foldables right in their portfolios.
- Additional Foldables templates can be found on pages R2–R6 of your Teacher Edition.

Assessment Solutions

- **McGraw-Hill networks™**
  Safe online testing features multiple question types that are easy to use and editable!
- **Self-Check Quizzes**
- **Worksheets**

UNIT 5 **At a Glance**

Lesson	Essential Question	Vocabulary	Digital Resources
1 Meeting People's Needs Pages 134–139	**How do people meet their needs?**	consumer consumer demand limited resource *community	Go to **connected.mcgraw-hill.com** for additional resources: • Interactive Whiteboard Lessons • Worksheets • Assessment • Lesson Plans • Content Library • Skill Builders • Videos • Use Standards Tracker on **networks** to track students' progress
2 Nations Trade Pages 140–143	**How do nations work together?**	trade *nation	
3 Making Choices About Money Pages 144–147	**Why do we make choices?**	benefit cost *personal *choice	

*denotes academic vocabulary

Introduce the Unit

✔ Diagnostic Assessment

Engage students in a discussion about the things they need to live.

Ask: *How do you get the things you need?*

After the discussion, show students the following pictures: a baker, a grocer, a doctor, and a builder. Have students tell what they know about each person's job. Then display the pictures in the four corners of the classroom.

Ask: *Where would you go to buy groceries?*

Have students point to the appropriate picture. Repeat with questions about the other pictures. Students' responses will help identify their level of understanding.

Explain to students that they made their choices based on how things are related to one another. For example, you would go to the baker for bread, the builder for a house, and the doctor's office for health care.

Say: *In this unit, you will learn more about how relationships affect your choices.*

Active Teaching

BIG IDEA **Relationships affect choices.**
In this unit about beginning economics, students will learn that relationships affect choices. Students will use the ***Show As You Go!*** pages throughout their study of this unit. Students will use information from each lesson to complete the activities.

At this point, have students fold back the corner of this page. This will help them flip back to this page as needed. Explain to students that at the end of the unit, they will use the information collected on these pages to complete the Big Idea Project.

Differentiated Instruction

▶ **Approaching** Review the directions with students and help define any unfamiliar words. After each lesson, allow students to work in a small group to complete the activity.

▶ **Beyond** Have students check their captions for appropriate capitalization and punctuation.

▶ **ELL** Have students circle key words in the directions. Define unfamiliar words for students. As lessons are completed, have students work with a partner to discuss and record information on the pages.

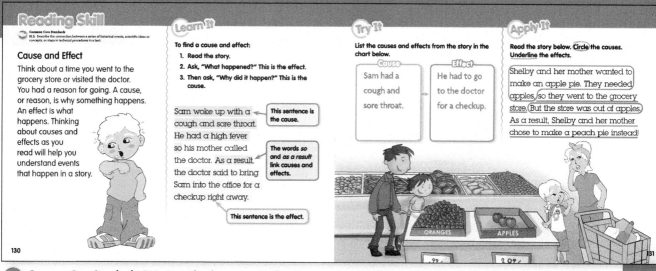

Common Core Standards
RI.3: Describe the connection between a series of historical events, scientific ideas or concepts, or steps in technical procedures in a text.

Cause and Effect

Think about a time you went to the grocery store or visited the doctor. You had a reason for going. A cause, or reason, is why something happens. An effect is what happens. Thinking about causes and effects as you read will help you understand events that happen in a story.

Learn It

To find a cause and effect:
1. Read the story.
2. Ask, "What happened?" This is the effect.
3. Then ask, "Why did it happen?" This is the cause.

Sam woke up with a cough and sore throat. He had a high fever so his mother called the doctor. As a result, the doctor said to bring Sam into the office for a checkup right away.

> This sentence is the cause.

> The words *so* and *as a result* link causes and effects.

> This sentence is the effect.

Try It

List the causes and effects from the story in the chart below.

Cause	Effect
Sam had a cough and sore throat.	He had to go to the doctor for a checkup.

Apply It

Read the story below. Circle the causes. Underline the effects.

Shelby and her mother wanted to make an apple pie. They needed apples, so they went to the grocery store. But the store was out of apples. As a result, Shelby and her mother chose to make a peach pie instead!

130   131

Common Core Standards RI.3: Describe the connection between a series of historical events, scientific ideas or concepts, or steps in technical procedures in a text.

Reading Skill

Active Teaching

⒧EARN IT Cause and Effect

Read page 128 together. Discuss the definitions of cause and effect. Share the following strategy for identifying cause and effect.

Say: *As I read, I think, "What is happening in the story and why?" This strategy helps me to identify the cause and effect. Being able to identify cause and effect helps me to understand how events in the story are connected.*

⒯RY IT Encourage students to try the modeled strategy as they complete the TRY IT activity.

⒜PPLY IT Have students complete the APPLY IT activity.

Ask:

1. *What two questions should you ask yourself to find the cause and effect of a story?* (What happened and why did it happen?) **L1**

2. *How can you tell which sentences in a story are the effects?* (The sentences that tell what happened are the effects. You can also look for the words *so*, *because*, and *as a result*.) **L2**

3. *Why is it important to identify the cause and effect of a story?* **L3**

Differentiated Instruction

▶ **Approaching** Review the LEARN IT activity as a small group. Do the TRY IT activity together. Have students complete the APPLY IT activity independently. Re-group to compare and correct.

▶ **Beyond** Have students add more events to each story. Have them circle the causes and underline the effects of the events they added.

▶ **ELL** Have students dramatize the stories on pages 128 and 129. Engage students in a discussion about what happened in each story. Explain that *what happened* is the *effect*. Discuss why the events in each story happened. Explain that *the reason something happened* is called the *cause*. Have students state cause and effect sentences about the story. Encourage them to use the words *because, so,* and *as a result* when they explain the effect.

netw⊙rks

Go to **connected.mcgraw-hill.com** for additional resources:
- Skill Builders
- Graphic Organizers

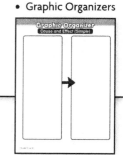

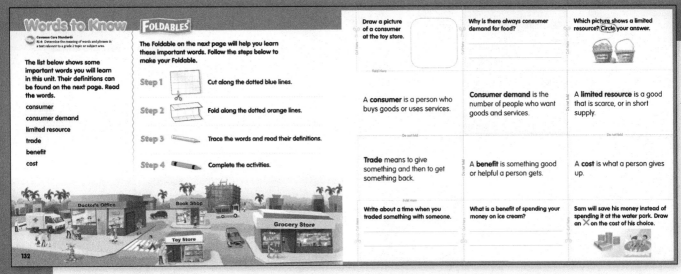

Common Core Standards RI.4: Determine the meaning of words and phrases in a text relevant to a grade 2 topic or subject area.

Words to Know
Active Teaching

1. Go to connected.mcgraw-hill.com for flashcards to introduce the unit vocabulary to students.

2. Read the words on the list on page 130 and have students repeat them after you.

3. Guide students as they complete steps 1 through 4 of the Foldable.

4. Have students use the Foldable to practice the vocabulary words independently or with a partner.

netw@rks

Go to connected.mcgraw-hill.com for additional resources:

- Vocabulary Flashcards
- Vocabulary Games
- Graphic Organizers

GO Vocabulary!

Use the graphic organizer below to help students practice the meanings of the words from the list. Model for students how to complete the graphic organizer using the word *trade*. Have students complete the graphic organizer for the other words independently or with a partner.

Definition to give something and then to get something back	**Description (in own words)** to exchange one thing for another

Word trade

Examples (from own life) trade sports cards trade lunch items	**Non-Examples** to give something away and get nothing in return

FOLDABLES®

Fold Here

Fold Here

Newspapers are a type of primary source. Newspapers can help us learn about what life was like in the past. This grocery ad is from a newspaper that was printed in 1950. That is more than 60 years ago!

Most people use newer technology, such as the Internet, to find their news today.

DBQ Document-Based Questions

1. Look at the ad on the right. How much money did three tall cans of milk cost in 1950?

   Three tall cans of milk cost 28 cents in 1950.

2. What does this grocery ad tell us about life in 1950?

networks
There's More Online!
Skill Builders
Resource Library

135

Differentiated Instruction

▶ **ELL** Dramatize a consumer buying something at a store.

Say: *I am a consumer. A consumer is a person who buys food and other things.*

Have students repeat the word *consumer*. Have students describe a time when they were consumers. Repeat the activity with the other words from the list.

W O R D P L A Y

Play Wordo to help students practice the vocabulary words on page 130.

• Print the Wordo card template from connected. mcgraw-hill.com. Make one copy per student and distribute to the class.

• Have students randomly write words from the list on page 130 in each square.

• Orally present a sentence or definition for each word on the list.

• Have students place counters or chips over the word that corresponds with the sentence or definition.

• A player wins when a vertical, horizontal, or diagonal line is covered.

When students are comfortable with the game, you may choose to have the students take turns calling out the definitions and sentences.

Active Teaching

Read page 133 together. Have students discuss what they notice about the newspaper advertisement pictured on the page. Then supply groups with advertisement pages from a daily newspaper. Have students compare newspaper advertisements from today with the one from 1950. Discuss how they are the same and different. Guide students through the written activities on the page. Discuss their responses.

Ask: *What can we learn about life in the past from newspaper ads?* **L3**

netw rks

Go to connected.mcgraw-hill.com for additional resources:

• Skill Builders   • Resource Library

Meeting People's Needs

Essential Question
How do people meet their needs?
What do you think?

Word Hunt
Find and circle these words.
*community
consumer
consumer demand
limited resource

Goods and Services

It was moving day for Sam and Shelby's family. They were moving from Grand Rapids, Michigan, to Charleston, South Carolina. Their new house was finally ready! Sam and Shelby were excited to be moving to their new home.

Sam and Shelby's family will need many things in their new **community**. They will buy goods and services to meet their needs. Goods are things that people grow or make to sell. Food and clothing are goods. Services are jobs that are done to help others. Doctors, teachers, and builders provide services.

GLUE FOLDABLE HERE

Sam and Shelby went shopping at the mall to buy some goods. They made a bar graph of what they bought.

- hats
- shirts
- belts
- shorts

A bar graph uses bars to display and compare information.

How many more hats than pairs of shorts did Sam and Shelby buy?

Lesson 1

Activate Prior Knowledge

Engage students in a discussion about moving to a new place.

Ask: *What kinds of things do people need when they move to a new place? How do people get the things they need?*

Explain that in this lesson, students will learn about how people meet their needs.

? Essential Question   How do people meet their needs?

Have students explain what they understand about the Essential Question. Discuss their responses. Explain that everything they learn in this lesson will help them understand the Essential Question better. Remind them to think about how the Essential Question connects to the unit Big Idea: Relationships affect choices

Page Power

FOLDABLES   Interact more with the page. Have students create a Notebook Foldable to assist them in developing their understanding that people supply goods and services based on consumer demand.

1. Provide students with a copy of Foldable 5A from the Notebook Foldables section at the back of this book.

2. Have students construct the Foldable and glue its anchor tab at the top of page 135.

3. On the Foldable flaps, have students write the definition of goods and services.

4. Under each flap, have students write the names of people and places that supply goods or services.

Active Teaching

Words To Know   Have students look through the lesson to find the words that are listed in the Word Hunt. Then have them read the definitions of the content vocabulary words and use context clues or the glossary to determine the meaning of the academic vocabulary word. Next have students name places in their community where consumers buy things they need.

Develop Comprehension

Tell students that they will be reading a story about a family that has moved to a different state. As they read, have students relate the story to their own lives. Read and discuss pages 134 and 135 together. Have students complete the activities on page 135. Discuss their responses.

Ask:

1. *What will Shelby and Sam's family need in their new community?* **L1**
2. *Where will they get the things they need?* **L2**
3. *How is your family like Sam and Shelby's family?* **L3**

Differentiated Instruction

▶ **ELL** Reread the sentences where the vocabulary words appear in the lesson. Have students point to the images that show consumers, consumer demand, and limited resources. Then ask students to describe the vocabulary in their own words.

Circle the consumers in the picture. Draw a **box** around the people and places that supply goods or services.

1. How do doctors meet consumers' needs?

   Doctors provide health care for consumers.

2. How do grocery stores meet consumers' needs?

3. How do builders meet consumers' needs?

   Builders provide housing for consumers.

THINK · PAIR · SHARE
Who supplies goods and services in your community?

Reading Skill
Use Visuals **Study the picture above. Underline the sentence that tells what the consumers in the picture are doing.**

Consumer Demand

The next day, Sam and Shelby went to their new doctor for a checkup. Then they went shopping at the market for the things they needed. Sam, Shelby, and their parents are **consumers**. Consumers, or buyers, are people who buy goods and services.

There are many consumers in a community. **Consumer demand** is the number of people who need goods and services. Consumers need things like food, health care, and housing. Sellers will buy these goods and services from people and businesses in the community.

138

139

Active Teaching

Read pages 136 and 137 together. Ask students to list goods or services that would be needed by many people. Engage students in a discussion about where people go to meet their needs. Then guide students as they complete the written activities. Discuss their responses.

Develop Comprehension

Ask:

1. *Why are the characters in the story consumers?* (They buy goods and services.) **L2**

2. *What is consumer demand?* (the number of people who need goods and services) **L1**

3. *Why are people who supply goods and services important to the community?* **L3**

Use the leveled reader, *From the Farm,* to extend and enrich students' understanding of goods and services. A lesson plan for this leveled reader can be found on pages T30–T31 at the front of this Teacher Edition.

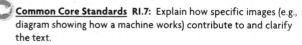 **Common Core Standards** RI.7: Explain how specific images (e.g., diagram showing how a machine works) contribute to and clarify the text.

Use the Visual For additional practice, have students describe what is happening in each place in the visual on pages 136 and 137. Have them discuss with partners or with as a class.

Differentiated Instruction

▶ **Approaching** Play a game where you state various needs of consumers and students name the people who meet those needs. Guide students to the conclusion that people supply goods and services to meet consumers' needs.

▶ **Beyond** Have students brainstorm a list of needs and name people in the community who meet those needs.

▶ **ELL** Have students point to and name the people who supply goods and services in the picture on pages 136 and 137. Discuss together how each person helps meet consumers' needs. Write students' answers on the board and read them together.

Resources

To make goods and provide services, people need three kinds of resources.

Natural resources are materials that come directly from nature. Water, soil, wood, and coal are all natural resources. Farmers use natural resources to grow goods.

Capital resources are goods made by people and used to make other goods and services. Factories, computers, trucks, hammers, and lawn mowers are all capital resources.

natural resource · capital resource · human resource

Human resources are people working to make goods and services. Painters, miners, and builders are examples of human resources. So are farmers and teachers. Human resources are important because every workplace needs workers.

What are natural, capital, and human resources?

Draw a resource that is important to you.

140

141

Lesson 1

Active Teaching

Read the pages together. Ask students to give examples of natural, capital, and human resources that they know of and see in their community.

Ask:

1. *Why are human resources necessary?* (They are needed to make goods, to provide services, and to do other kinds of work.) **L2**

2. *What would happen if there was a shortage of resources?* (Answers will vary but may include that services would be left undone and goods could not be made.) **L3**

3. *How do capital resources differ from natural resources?* (Capital resources are used to make another good or service. Natural resources are used just as they are.) **L3**

4. *What would happen if an economy did not have any capital resources?* (The economy could not produce as many goods and would not be as strong.) **L3**

Differentiated Instruction

▶ **Approaching** Reread the lesson with students, using the section headings to pose questions to assess their understanding.

▶ **Beyond** Have students come up with a business plan to address a good or service not currently provided to their community.

▶ **ELL** Write *natural resources, human resources,* and *capital resources* on the board. Have students draw a picture to represent each type of resource.

networks

Go to **connected.mcgraw-hill.com** for additional resources:
- Interactive Whiteboard Lessons
- Worksheets
- Assessment

Graphic Organizer
Cause and Effect (Simple)

Limited Resources

Shelby and her mother went to the grocery store to buy apples to make apple pie. But the bin for apples was almost empty. The few apples that were left also cost more money than the other fruits.

When there is not enough of a good, we say that it is a **limited resource**. A limited resource is a good that is scarce, or in short supply.

People have to make choices because of limited resources. They may choose to pay more money for a limited resource, or they may shop somewhere else. They may decide to buy something different or nothing at all.

142

143

Active Teaching

Read pages 138 and 139 together. Ask students to describe a time when something they wanted to buy was a limited resource.

Ask: *What choice did you make because the good was a limited resource?*

Guide students through the written activities. Discuss their responses.

Develop Comprehension

Ask:

1. *What is a limited resource?* (a good that is scarce or in short supply) **L1**

2. *What choices do people have when the good they want to buy is a limited resource?* (They can pay more, shop elsewhere, or buy something else.) **L2**

3. *Why do people have to make choices because of limited resources?* **L3**

Summarize the lesson with the class. Then have students respond to the Essential Question. Discuss their responses. Have students revisit their response on page 134 and compare it to their response at the end of the lesson. Discuss how their answers changed.

> *Show As You Go!* Remind students to go back to the Unit Opener and complete the activities for this lesson.

Reading Skill

🌀 **Common Core Standards** RI.1: Ask and answer such questions as *who, what, where, when, why,* and *how* to demonstrate understanding of key details in a text.

Ask and Answer Questions about Key Details
For additional practice, ask students to think of a question to ask a partner about the lesson. Have partners ask and answer each other's questions.

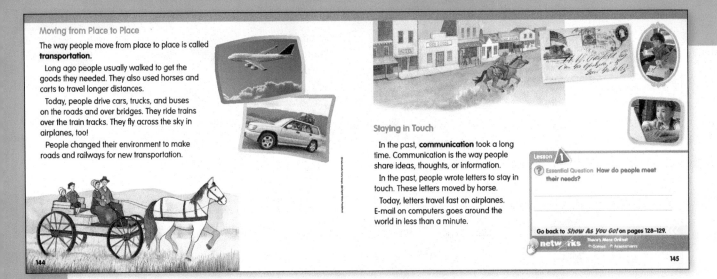

Moving from Place to Place

The way people move from place to place is called **transportation.**

Long ago people usually walked to get the goods they needed. They also used horses and carts to travel longer distances.

Today, people drive cars, trucks, and buses on the roads and over bridges. They ride trains over the train tracks. They fly across the sky in airplanes, too!

People changed their environment to make roads and railways for new transportation.

Staying in Touch

In the past, **communication** took a long time. Communication is the way people share ideas, thoughts, or information.

In the past, people wrote letters to stay in touch. These letters moved by horse.

Today, letters travel fast on airplanes. E-mail on computers goes around the world in less than a minute.

Lesson 1
? Essential Question How do people meet their needs?

Go back to *Show As You Go!* on pages 128–129.

net w rks

144

145

Lesson 1

Active Teaching

Read the pages together. Ask students to describe what they already know about transportation and communication.

Ask students to look at the pictures on the pages. How are they different? How are they the same?

Develop Comprehension

Ask:

1. *What do the pictures show?* (Images of past and present transportation and communication.) **L1**

2. *How is transportation different from the past to today?* (Transportation was slow in the past and much quicker and efficient today.) **L2**

3. *How is communication different from the past to today?* (Communication took days via letters; today it is instant with computers and telephones.) **L2**

Summarize the lesson with the class. Then have students respond to the Essential Question. Discuss their responses. Have students revisit their response on the page and compare it with their response at the end of the lesson. Discuss how their answers changed.

> ***Show As You Go!*** Remind students to go back to the Unit Opener and complete the activities for this lesson.

Response to Intervention

? **Essential Question** **How do people meet their needs?**

If . . . students cannot give a substantiated response to the Essential Question, "How do people meet their needs?"

. . . .

Then . . . take students back to pages 134 through 139. Discuss how Sam and Shelby's family met their needs for food, housing, and health care.

Ask: *How do people in your family meet their needs?*

Following the discussion, allow students to respond to the Essential Question again.

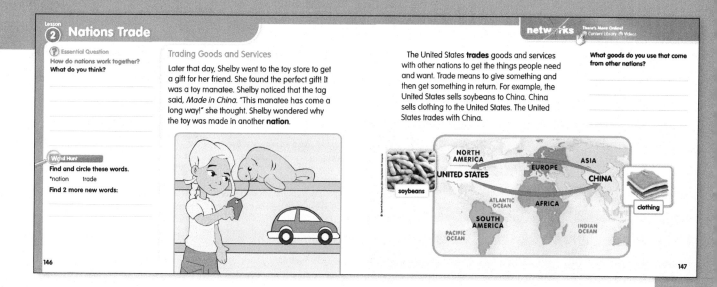

Lesson
2 **Nations Trade**

netw**rks** There's More Online!
Content Library Videos

Essential Question
How do nations work together?
What do you think?

Word Hunt
Find and circle these words.
*nation   trade
Find 2 more new words:

Trading Goods and Services

Later that day, Shelby went to the toy store to get a gift for her friend. She found the perfect gift! It was a toy manatee. Shelby noticed that the tag said, *Made in China.* "This manatee has come a long way!" she thought. Shelby wondered why the toy was made in another **nation**.

The United States **trades** goods and services with other nations to get the things people need and want. Trade means to give something and then get something in return. For example, the United States sells soybeans to China. China sells clothing to the United States. The United States trades with China.

What goods do you use that come from other nations?

NORTH AMERICA
UNITED STATES
soybeans
ATLANTIC OCEAN
SOUTH AMERICA
PACIFIC OCEAN
EUROPE
ASIA
CHINA
clothing
AFRICA
INDIAN OCEAN

146

147

Lesson 2

Activate Prior Knowledge

Say: *Did you know that many of the goods we use in the United States come from other countries?*

Ask: *How can you find out where a good was made?*

Supply a bag of various goods, some made in the United States and some made in other nations. Have students look for the words that say "Made in..." and tell where the goods were made.

Say: *This activity helped you to see that some of the goods and services we use come from other nations.*

Explain to students that in this unit they will be learning how the United States trades with other nations to exchange goods and services.

(?) **Essential Question How do nations work together?**

Have students explain what they understand about the Essential Question. Discuss their responses. Explain that everything they learn in this lesson will help them understand the Essential Question better. Remind them to think about how the Essential Question connects to the unit Big Idea: Relationships affect choices

Active Teaching

Words To Know Have students look through the lesson to find the words that are listed in the Word Hunt. Then have them read the definitions of the content vocabulary words and use context clues or the glossary to determine the meaning of the academic vocabulary word. Next have partners role play trading items in the classroom.

Say: *Our nation is called the United States.*

Ask students to name the nations that are north and south of the United States.

Develop Comprehension
Read pages 140 and 141 together. Guide students through the written activities. Discuss their responses.

Ask:

1. *What does* trade *mean?* (to give something and get something in return) **L1**

2. *What are examples of goods and services that the United States trades with other nations?* **L2**

3. *Why do nations trade with each other?* (to get things we need) **L2**

Differentiated Instruction

▶ **ELL** Use the Internet with students to research goods and services from their home countries that are sold in the United States. Find out what goods and services the United States exports to their home countries.

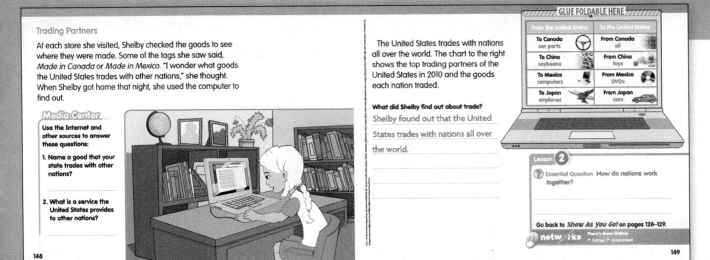

Trading Partners

At each store she visited, Shelby checked the goods to see where they were made. Some of the tags she saw said, *Made in Canada* or *Made in Mexico*. "I wonder what goods the United States trades with other nations," she thought. When Shelby got home that night, she used the computer to find out.

Media Center

Use the Internet and other sources to answer these questions:

1. Name a good that your state trades with other nations?

2. What is a service the United States provides to other nations?

The United States trades with nations all over the world. The chart to the right shows the top trading partners of the United States in 2010 and the goods each nation traded.

What did Shelby find out about trade?

Shelby found out that the United States trades with nations all over the world.

From the United States	To the United States
To Canada — car parts	From Canada — oil
To China — soybeans	From China — toys
To Mexico — computers	From Mexico — DVDs
To Japan — airplanes	From Japan — cars

Lesson 2

? Essential Question How do nations work together?

Go back to *Show As You Go!* on pages 128–129.

Lesson 2

Active Teaching

Read pages 142 and 143 together. Locate the top trading partners of the United States on a wall map. Discuss the goods that each nation trades. Guide students through the written activities and discuss their responses.

Visit the media center with students. Have partners use the Internet and other sources to find answers to the questions on page 142.

Summarize the lesson with the class. Then have students respond to the Essential Question. Have students revisit their response on page 140 and compare it to their response at the end of the lesson. Discuss how their answers changed.

Show As You Go! Remind students to go back to the Unit Opener and complete the activities for this lesson.

Page Power

FOLDABLES Interact more with the page. Have students create a Notebook Foldable to assist them in developing their understanding of trade.

1. Provide students with a copy of Foldable 5B from the Notebook Foldables section at the back of this book.

2. Have students construct the Foldable and glue its anchor tab above the chart on page 143.

3. On the Foldable flaps, have students write "United States" and the names of the two nations that trade with the United States (one name on each flap).

4. On the backs of the flaps, have students draw and label a good or service that each nation trades.

Response to Intervention

? Essential Question How do nations work together?

If . . . students cannot give a substantiated response to the Essential Question, "How do nations work together?"

Then . . . display the goods that were used in the Activate Prior Knowledge activity. Have students recall that some of the goods were made in other nations. Ask students to describe what they learned about trade from the map and chart in Lesson 2. Following the discussion, allow students to respond to the Essential Question again.

networks

Go to connected.mcgraw-hill.com for additional resources:
- Interactive Whiteboard Lessons
- Assessment
- Worksheets

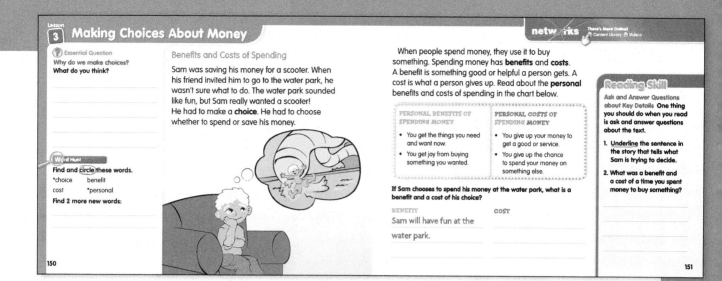

Lesson
3 Making Choices About Money

netw⊕rks There's More Online!
Content Library Videos

Essential Question
Why do we make choices?
What do you think?

Word Hunt
Find and circle these words.
*choice   benefit
cost   *personal
Find 2 more new words:

Benefits and Costs of Spending

Sam was saving his money for a scooter. When his friend invited him to go to the water park, he wasn't sure what to do. The water park sounded like fun, but Sam really wanted a scooter! He had to make a **choice**. He had to choose whether to spend or save his money.

When people spend money, they use it to buy something. Spending money has **benefits** and **costs**. A benefit is something good or helpful a person gets. A cost is what a person gives up. Read about the **personal** benefits and costs of spending in the chart below.

PERSONAL BENEFITS OF SPENDING MONEY	PERSONAL COSTS OF SPENDING MONEY
• You get the things you need and want now.	• You give up your money to get a good or service.
• You get joy from buying something you wanted.	• You give up the chance to spend your money on something else.

If Sam chooses to spend his money at the water park, what is a benefit and a cost of his choice?

BENEFIT
Sam will have fun at the water park.

COST

Reading Skill

Ask and Answer Questions about Key Details One thing you should do when you read is ask and answer questions about the text.

1. Underline the sentence in the story that tells what Sam is trying to decide.

2. What was a benefit and a cost of a time you spent money to buy something?

150

151

Lesson 3

Activate Prior Knowledge

Draw a piggy bank on chart paper.

Say: *Imagine we have ten dollars in our classroom piggy bank.*

Ask: *How do you think we should use our money?*

List students' responses on chart paper. Engage the class in a discussion about whether to use the money now or later.

Say: *In this lesson, we will learn about making choices about money. As we read the lesson, we will return to this chart to see if you have changed your decision about how to use the money.*

? Essential Question Why do we make choices?

Have students explain what they understand about the Essential Question. Discuss their responses. Explain that everything they learn in this lesson will help them understand the Essential Question better. Remind them to think about how the Essential Question connects to the unit Big Idea: Relationships affect choices

Active Teaching

Words To Know Have students look through the lesson to find the words that are listed in the Word Hunt. Then have them read the definitions of the content vocabulary words and use context clues or the glossary to determine the meaning of the academic vocabulary words. Next have students describe a time when they had to make a choice about something. Then have students name things in the classroom that are their personal property.

Develop Comprehension

Read pages 144 and 145 together. Guide students through the written activities. Have students share their responses.

Ask:

1. *What are the benefits of spending the money we have in our classroom piggy bank?* **L2**

2. *What are the costs of spending the money we have in our classroom piggy bank?* **L2**

3. *Why is it important to think about the costs and benefits of spending our money?* **L3**

Differentiated Instruction

▶ **ELL** To help students understand the costs and benefits of spending money, write the following sentence frames on the board:

A benefit of spending our money on pizza is _____.

A cost of spending on money on pizza is _____.

Have students take turns finishing the sentences. Replace the word *pizza* with other goods and services and repeat the activity.

Benefits and Costs of Saving

Like spending, saving money also has benefits and costs. Read about the personal benefits and costs of saving in the chart on the next page. Then help Sam decide whether to keep saving his money for a scooter or spend it at the water park.

THINK • PAIR • SHARE
What do you think Sam should do? Why?

PERSONAL BENEFITS OF SAVING MONEY	PERSONAL COSTS OF SAVING MONEY
• You have more money for something you need and want.	• You give up spending your money now.
• Saving helps you plan for the future.	• You have to wait until later to enjoy the benefit of a good or service.

You can buy goods using a credit card, check, debit card, or money order.

Think about a time when you saved your money to buy something. What was a benefit of your choice to save? What was a cost?

_____

_____

_____

Lesson 3

? Essential Question Why do we make choices?

_____

_____

_____

Go back to *Show As You Go!* on pages 128–129.

Lesson 3

Active Teaching

Read and discuss pages 146 and 147. Guide students as they complete the written activities. After partners engage in the Think, Pair, Share activity, have volunteers share what they would do if they were Sam and why.

Develop Comprehension

Ask:

1. *What are the benefits and costs of saving money?* **L1**

2. *How does saving money help you plan for the future?* **L2**

3. *What can we do to make wise choices with our money?* (We have to think about the benefits and costs of saving or spending before we make a decision.) **L3**

Revisit the chart with the piggy bank.

Ask: *What should we do with our classroom money? What are the benefits and costs of your choice?*

Summarize the lesson with the class. Then have students respond to the Essential Question. Discuss their responses. Have students revisit their response on page 144 and compare it to their response at the end of the lesson. Discuss how their answers changed.

Show As You Go! Remind students to go back to complete the project on the Unit Opener.

Response to Intervention

? **Essential Question How do we make choices?**

If . . . students cannot give a substantiated response to the Essential Question, "How do we make choices?"

. . . .

Then . . . discuss the choice that Sam needed to make in the story. Ask students to tell what Sam had to think about before making his decision. Then have each student describe how he or she made their decision to use the classroom money. Following the discussion, allow students to respond to the Essential Question again.

networks

Go to **connected.mcgraw-hill.com** for additional resources:

- Interactive Whiteboard Lessons
- Assessment
- Videos
- Worksheets

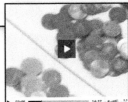

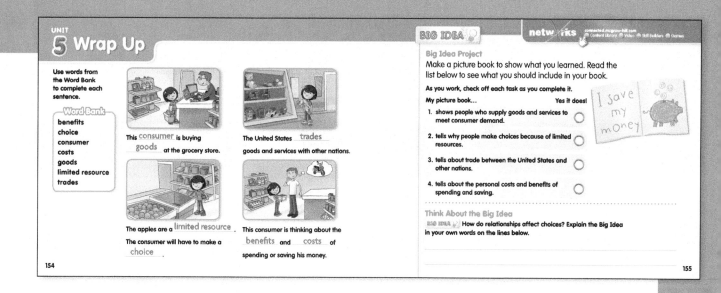

Wrap Up

Comic Strip

Have students look at the pictures and read the sentences. Then have them choose a word from the Word Bank to complete each sentence.

 **Big Idea Project**

Students will be making a book to show what they learned in Unit 5.

1. Read the checklist together and answer any questions students may have about the project.

2. Stock the writing center with paper, pencils, magazines, and art materials.

3. Have students take part in the following process: brainstorm ideas, write a rough draft, take part in a peer review, revise the rough draft, and write/illustrate a final copy.

4. Have students sit in the Author's Chair as they read their books to the class.

Differentiated Instruction

▶ **Approaching** Have students draw pictures for each page of their books. Ask them to describe what is happening in each picture. Write their words. Help students practice reading their books.

▶ **Beyond** Have students add additional details to explain what is happening in their pictures.

▶ **ELL** Have students label their pages with the following headings: Goods and Services; Limited Resources; Trade; and Saving and Spending. Have students discuss personal experiences with each topic. Then have them write and illustrate each topic. Have students practice reading their books to a classmate.

Response to Intervention

BIG IDEA Relationships affect choices.

If . . . students cannot give a substantiated response to the Big Idea, "Relationships affect choices"

Then . . . have students think about the choices the characters made in each lesson. Ask students to describe what influenced each character's decisions. Point out the relationships that were addressed in each lesson, for example: Where did Sam and Shelby's family go to meet their needs? Why did the toy Shelby bought come from another nation? What did Sam think about before he used his money? Following the discussion, allow students to respond to the Big Idea again.

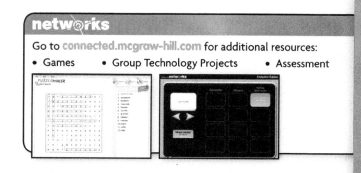

netw⚙rks

Go to connected.mcgraw-hill.com for additional resources:
- Games
- Group Technology Projects
- Assessment

Name _____ Date _____

Economics Book Rubric

4 Exemplary	3 Accomplished	2 Developing	1 Beginning
The picture book:	**The picture book:**	**The picture book:**	**The picture book:**
☐ accurately uses words and pictures to explain how people supply goods and services based on consumer demand	☐ has mostly accurate words and pictures to explain how people supply goods and services based on consumer demand	☐ has somewhat accurate words and pictures to explain how people supply goods and services based on consumer demand	☐ has few accurate words and pictures to explain how people supply goods and services based on consumer demand
☐ accurately uses words and pictures to explain why people make choices because of limited resources	☐ has mostly accurate words and pictures to explain how people make choices because of limited resources	☐ has some accurate words and pictures to explain how people make choices because of limited resources	☐ has few accurate words and pictures to explain how people make choices because of limited resources
☐ accurately uses words and pictures to explain trade between the United States and other nations	☐ has mostly accurate words and pictures to explain trade between the United States and other nations	☐ has some accurate words and pictures to explain trade between the United States and other nations	☐ has few accurate words and pictures to explain trade between the United States and other nations
☐ accurately uses words and pictures to explain the benefits and costs of spending and saving	☐ has mostly accurate words and pictures to explain the benefits and costs of spending and saving	☐ has some accurate words and pictures to explain the benefits and costs of spending and saving	☐ has few accurate words and pictures to explain the benefits and costs of spending and saving
☐ contains few, if any, errors in grammar, punctuation, capitalization, and spelling	☐ contains some errors in grammar, punctuation, capitalization, and spelling	☐ contains several errors in grammar, punctuation, capitalization, and spelling	☐ contains serious errors in grammar, punctuation, capitalization, and spelling

Grading Comments: _____

_____

_____

_____

_____

Project Score: _____

Teacher Notes

Picture Glossary

B

*belief   A **belief** is what someone believes to be true.

benefit   A **benefit** is something good or helpful a person gets .

*blend   To **blend** means to mix together completely.

C

*choice   A **choice** is when a person picks one thing over another.

citizen   A **citizen** is a person who belongs to a country.

colonist   A **colonist** is a person who travels to a new land to settle it.

colony   A **colony** is a place that is ruled by another country.

*community   A **community** is a place where people live, work, and play.

compass rose   A **compass rose** shows the four cardinal directions and the four intermediate directions.

Constitution   The **Constitution** is a plan for our government.

consumer   A **consumer** is a person who buys goods and uses services.

Picture Glossary

consumer demand **Consumer demand** is the number of people who need goods and services.

contribution A **contribution** is the act of giving or doing something.

cost A **cost** is what a person gives up.

crops **Crops** are plants people grow for food or other uses.

culture **Culture** is the way a group of people live. It is made up of a group's special food, music, and art.

158

Picture Glossary

custom A **custom** is a special way of doing something that is shared by many people.

D

desert A **desert** is a large area of very dry land.

E

*element An **element** is one part of something.

Ellis Island **Ellis Island** was an important immigration center in the United States.

*equal **Equal** means that something is the same as something else.

159

Picture Glossary

Equator The **Equator** is an imaginary line around the middle of Earth.

*escape To **escape** means to get free or run away from danger.

F

*force To **force** means to cause someone to do something against their wishes.

*function A **function** is a use or purpose.

G

*gather To **gather** means to collect.

globe A **globe** is a round model of the Earth.

160

[R]The Granger Collection, NY

---

government A **government** is all of the people who run a community, state, or country.

governor A **governor** is the leader of our state.

H

*herd A **herd** is a group of animals that live or travel together.

I

*imaginary **Imaginary** means not real.

immigrant An **immigrant** is a person who leaves one country to live in another.

intermediate directions The **intermediate directions** are the directions in between the cardinal directions. They are northeast, northwest, southeast, and southwest.

[R]Edmund Van Hoorick/Getty Images

161

*introduce   To **introduce** means to present formally.

L

*level   A **level** is a floor of a building.

limited resource   A **limited resource** is a good that is scarce, or in short supply.

M

map key   A **map key**, or map legend, tells what the pictures on a map mean.

map scale   A **map scale** shows how far apart places really are on a map.

*material   A **material** is a thing needed to make something.

mayor   A **mayor** is the leader of our community.

N

*nation   A **nation** is a particular land where people live.

naturalization   **Naturalization** is when a person becomes a citizen of another country.

natural resource   **Natural resources** are materials found in nature that people use.

North Pole   The very top of the Earth is called the **North Pole**.

Picture Glossary

*personal **Personal** means relating to a particular person.

physical map A **physical map** shows different land and water features like mountains, rivers, lakes, and oceans.

political map A **political map** shows the borders of states, countries, and other areas.

*positive **Positive** means good or helpful.

prairie A **prairie** is an area of flat land or rolling hills covered in grasses.

164

Picture Glossary

President The **President** is the leader of our country.

Prime Meridian The **Prime Meridian** is an imaginary line that runs from the North Pole to the South Pole.

recycle To **recycle** means to reuse something.

region A **region** is an area with common features that make it different from other areas.

*represent To **represent** means to serve as a sign or symbol for something.

165

Picture Glossary

responsible   **Responsible** means able to choose between right and wrong.

right   A **right** is a freedom that we have.

***rule**   To **rule** means to have power or control over someone.

Rural   **Rural** communities are far from cities.

 settlement   A **settlement** is a place that is newly set up as home.

Picture Glossary

South Pole   The very bottom of the Earth is called the **South Pole**.

South Pole

Statue of Liberty   The **Statue of Liberty** is a large statue in New York Harbor of a woman holding a torch.

suburban   **Suburban** communities are less crowded than urban areas.

Picture Glossary

*structure   **Structure** is the way parts are arranged.

symbol   A **symbol** is something that stands for something else.

T   thematic map   A **thematic map** tells us certain information about a place or area.

trade   To **trade** means to give something and then get something in return.

*travel   To **travel** means to go from one place to another.

U   Urban   A city, like New York, is an **urban** community.

V   veteran   A **veteran** is a person who has been in the military.

volunteer   A **volunteer** is a person who works for free to help others.

Index

This index lists many topics you can find in your book. It tells the page numbers on which they are found. If you see the letter *m* before a page number, you will find a map on that page.

Index

FOLDABLES® by Dinah Zike

Notebook Foldables®
Strategies for using your Networks Elementary Social Studies Program

- Help students organize information.

- Engage students further with the text.

- Provide an opportunity for enrichment and extension.

How to Construct Notebook Foldables®

Provide students with a copy of the template that corresponds to the activity you wish to teach. Then, direct students to:

1. **Fold** the anchor tab(s) and the information tabs where indicated on the template.
2. **Glue** the anchor tab(s) to the page where indicated.
3. **Cut** the Foldable to separate the information tab(s).

Once students have constructed their Notebook Foldables®, have them complete the activity as described in the Teacher Edition.

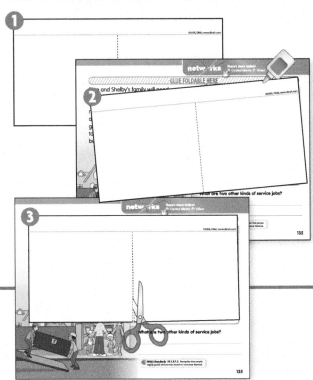

Notebook Foldables® by Dinah Zike

This best-selling book from Dinah Zike features adaptations of her Foldables® specially designed to fit into composition books, spiral notebooks, binders, and even Big Books. The book comes with reproducible graphics and instructions on how to create these modified Foldables® using regular paper. You'll be amazed at the hundreds of full-color examples found throughout the book! This book contains 129 pages complete with templates and a complimentary CD for easy customization and insertion of your own text and graphics.

For more information on this or other Dinah Zike products, visit www.dinah.com or call 1-800-99DINAH.

ISBN-10: 1-882796-27-6

Unit 1 Notebook FOLDABLES®

Fold and glue BEFORE cutting!

Notebook Foldables® 1A—Use with Unit 1 Lesson 2, page 19.

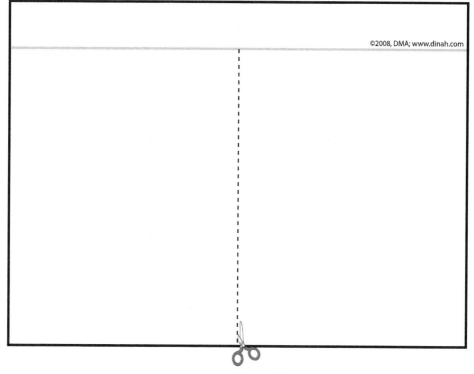

©2008, DMA; www.dinah.com

Notebook Foldables® 1B—Use with Unit 1 Lesson 3, page 22.

©2008, DMA; www.dinah.com

Fold and glue <u>BEFORE</u> cutting!

Notebook Foldables® 2A—Use with Unit 2 Lesson 3, page 44.

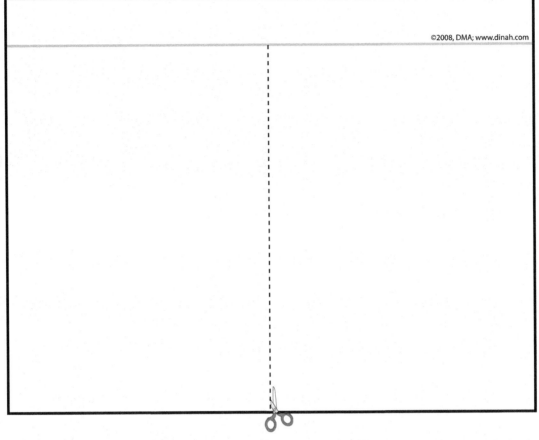

©2008, DMA; www.dinah.com

Notebook Foldables® 2B—Use with Unit 2 Lesson 5, page 53.

©2008, DMA; www.dinah.com

Fold and glue **BEFORE** cutting!

Notebook Foldables® 3A—Use with Unit 3 Lesson 2, page 76.

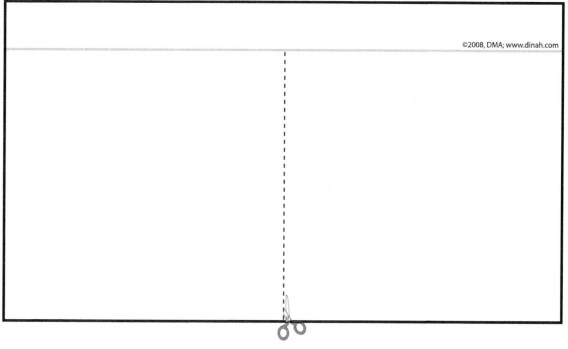

©2008, DMA; www.dinah.com

Notebook Foldables® 3B—Use with Unit 3 Lesson 3, page 81.

©2008, DMA; www.dinah.com

Unit 4 Notebook FOLDABLES®

Fold and glue BEFORE cutting!

Notebook Foldables® 4A—Use with Unit 4 Lesson 2, page 103.

©2008, DMA; www.dinah.com

Notebook Foldables® 4B—Use with Unit 4 Lesson 4, page 112.

©2008, DMA; www.dinah.com

Fold and glue BEFORE cutting!

Notebook Foldables® 5A—Use with Unit 5 Lesson 1, page 135.

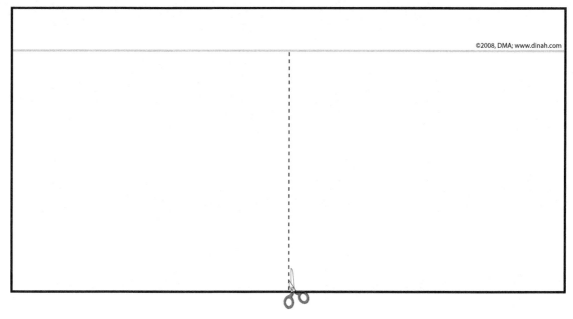

©2008, DMA; www.dinah.com

Notebook Foldables® 5B—Use with Unit 5 Lesson 2, page 143.

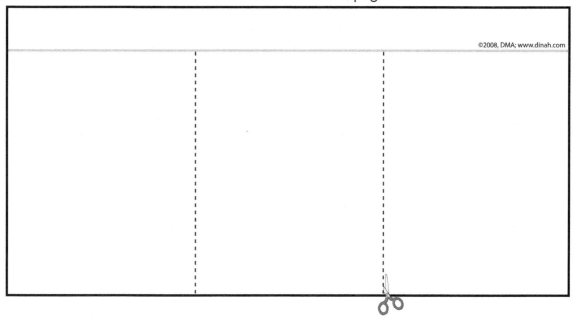

©2008, DMA; www.dinah.com

Teacher Notes